WELCOME

to the

MYSTERYVERSE

To Martin, whose curiosity and sense of wonder about the world never fails to inspire. – C.G.

For Bia and Ernie, and all the staff and pupils at George Tomlinson. – B.B.

To my Dad for all the many questions answered and to Tove and Kit for all the things we will learn together. – L.C.

First Published in 2023 by Wide Eyed Editions,
an imprint of The Quarto Group.
100 Cummings Center, Suite 265D, Beverly, MA 0195, USA.
T (978) 282-9590 F (978) 283-2742 www.Quarto.com

The illustrations were hand drawn with fine liner pen and colored digitally in Photoshop
Set in Brandon Grotesque, Juniper, Tango BT and P22 Mackinac Pro

Designer: Sasha Moxon
Editor: Corinne Lucas
Production Controller: Dawn Cameron
Art Director: Karissa Santos
Publisher: Debbie Foy and Georgia Buckthorn

Manufactured in Guangdong, China CC0723

9 8 7 6 5 4 3 2 1

FSC
MIX
Paper | Supporting responsible forestry
FSC® C008047

WELCOME to the MYSTERYVERSE

WRITTEN BY
Clive Gifford

ILLUSTRATED BY
Good Wives
and Warriors

WIDE EYED EDITIONS

CONTENTS

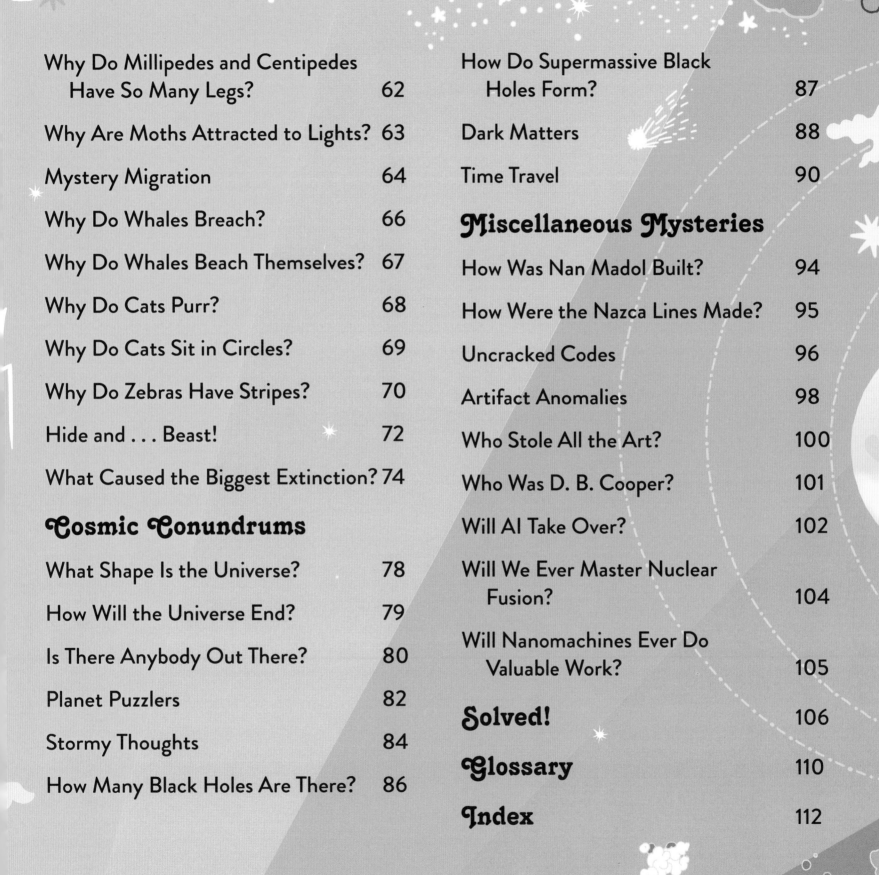

INTRODUCTION

Humans are a curious bunch. That's probably why you're reading this book! We're curious about EVERYTHING: ourselves, the things around us, other living creatures and what exists beyond our planet. This curiosity has led us to carry out incredible experiments, voyage around the world, explore new places and discover plants, creatures and natural phenomena. And it doesn't end there. Scientists and other bright sparks have achieved unimaginable things in their quest for answers to questions about how humans, Earth and even the universe works.

Our knowledge is constantly expanding and we understand more than ever before, yet incredibly there are still so many things we don't know. Why do we dream, yawn or have fingerprints? Where did all of Earth's water come from? How did life begin and how might the universe end? Do aliens exist? Is time travel possible? Why do cats purr? The list goes on and on and on . . .

So let's take a look at some of the most baffling and mysterious gaps in our knowledge, from people and nature to Earth and space and everything else in between. In this book you'll discover the latest theories and explanations for these unknown wonders. And find out what obstacles stand in our way of discovering the truth. Who knows, maybe we've already solved the riddles and we just need to prove the theories, or perhaps new ideas will explain the seemingly unexplainable. Or maybe, some things will remain in the Mysteryverse.

SOLVING THE UNKNOWN

As you read this, tens of thousands of scientists, engineers, technicians and curious minds are hard at work advancing human knowledge. They're using all sorts of tools, from their own creativity to massive machinery, to try to find answers to all of the unsolved questions in the Mysteryverse, and more puzzles besides.

Uncovering Fresh Evidence

Naturalists (people who study living things) scour the planet in search of new – and long-forgotten – species of plants and animals. Drones, underwater probes and land-monitoring satellites are used to chart changes to the environment. Getting beneath Earth's surface has also revealed many treasures, from unknown caves and fossils to ancient buried cities and artifacts. This work has advanced our knowledge, particularly about dinosaurs and other prehistoric life.

Turning To Tech

Advances in technology, especially powerful computers, have given scientists valuable new tools to solve problems. Computer modeling, for example, is used to simulate complicated real-world actions, such as winds in a storm or air over a speeding vehicle. These models allow scientists to investigate and understand complex processes and predict what comes next. Some models are helping scientists work out the precise impacts of climate change.

Carbon Dating

All living things absorb carbon until they die. One type of carbon (carbon 14) then starts to decay at a specific rate – half of it breaks down and disappears every 5,730 years. So, by measuring how much carbon 14 is left, scientists can date once-living objects, from shells and bones to materials such as paper, leather and wood. Carbon dating has helped solve many historical mysteries.

Seeing More Clearly

As scientific instruments have improved, they allow scientists to examine things in greater detail. Electron microscopes can view individual atoms, while powerful space telescopes, such as Hubble and James Webb, can spot objects in space that were once impossible to see. Such devices are increasing what we know about the universe.

Helicobacter pylori bacteria causes stomach ulcers.

Don't Try This At Home

There are moments when a scientist takes a leap of faith to prove their theory. Stomach ulcers were once thought to be caused by stress, spicy foods or too much acid, but Dr. Barry Marshall was convinced a bacteria was to blame. He added some to a broth and drank it! When he developed the very symptoms that ulcer patients suffer from, it proved his theory and led to treatments for many ulcers.

Lucky Break

Sometimes, chance or luck produces an accidental breakthrough. A dish containing bacteria in Alexander Fleming's lab in 1928 was left unwashed. A mold grew in the dish, which killed off the bacteria. This led to the discovery of the first antibiotic, penicillin. Antibiotics have saved countless lives by tackling harmful bacteria. And it's all thanks to an unwashed dish (and a very clever mind)!

PEOPLE PUZZLERS

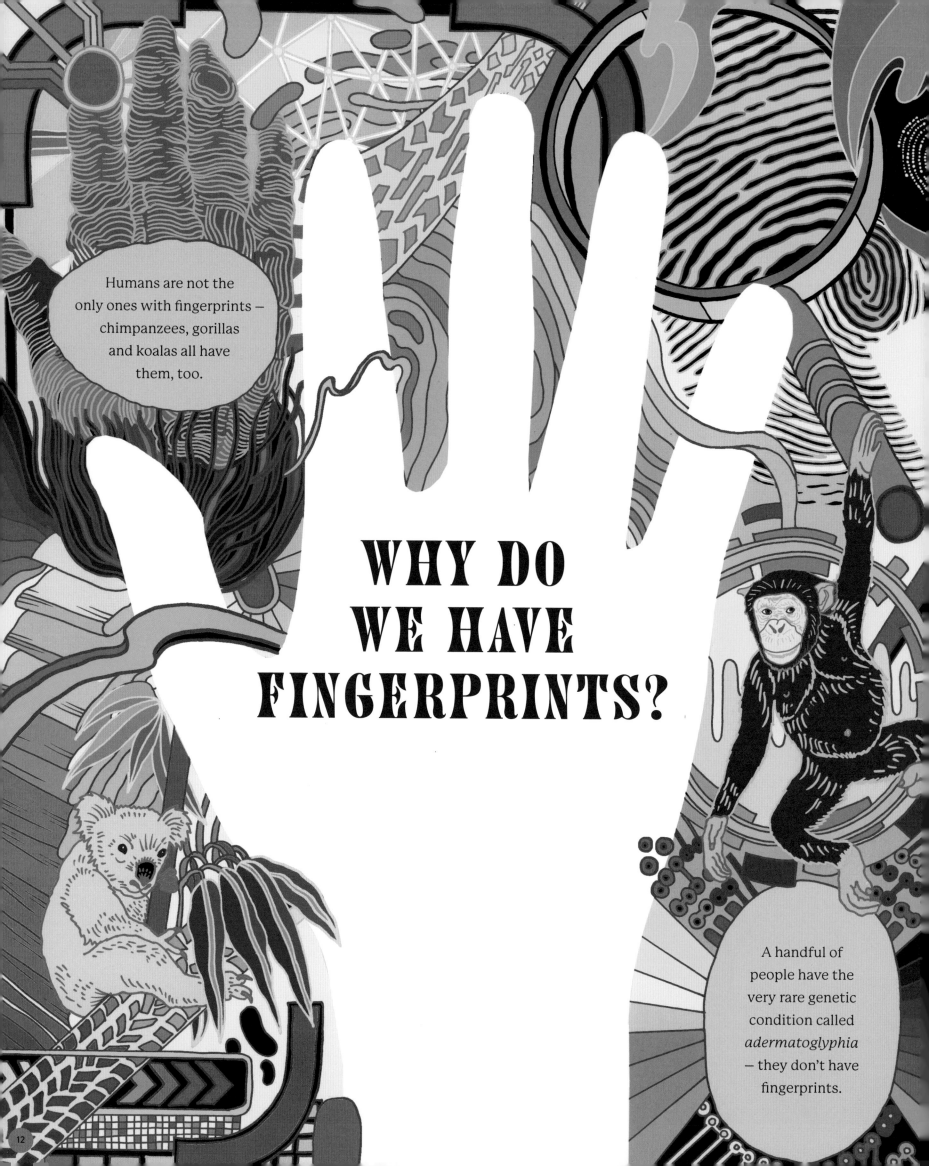

Humans are not the only ones with fingerprints – chimpanzees, gorillas and koalas all have them, too.

WHY DO WE HAVE FINGERPRINTS?

A handful of people have the very rare genetic condition called *adermatoglyphia* – they don't have fingerprints.

Every one of the eight billion people on Earth have fingerprints that are totally unique (except for the few who don't have fingerprints! Keep reading . . .). Those telltale markings on your fingertips are yours and yours alone – not even identical twins have the exact same ones. Made up of lots of tiny raised ridges and valleys, which form endlessly varied patterns known as loops, arches and whorls, your fingerprints are fully formed two or three months before you're born.

Get a Grip

Until recently, scientists thought that those tiny ridges and valleys helped people grip objects, a little like how the tread on a bike tire grips the ground. No one fully tested out this theory until 2009 when scientists discovered that fingerprints actually *reduce* how well you grip smooth objects because less of your fingertip's surface is touching the object. Suddenly, an alternative explanation was needed.

Slippery Solution

Some think fingerprints may still help with grip, but only with rough surfaces such as tree branches. Fingerprints may have evolved when humans still climbed and lived in trees. Could they have helped us keep hold of wet, slippery objects, such as rain-soaked tree trunks? Perhaps the grooves channel water away.

A Touching Theory

New research suggests fingerprints might increase the sensitivity of your sense of touch. Scientists found that the ridges of your fingerprints are crammed with more nerve cells than any other part of your body. These may allow your fingertips to detect and feel the finest textures and the slightest bumps on the surface of an object.

Tough Problem

Another theory is that they help toughen up our fingertips and stop them from getting blisters. Or maybe, it's a combination of some of these things. For the moment, we simply don't know and can only wonder why fingerprints are so unique to (almost) each and every one or us.

Handing Out Justice

Oil and sweat from fingertips leave a person's identity behind in the form of prints on smooth surfaces. These can be collected by law enforcement officers who compare them to sets of fingerprints stored in computer databases to search for a match.

YAWNING GAP

You don't just yawn when you need to go to bed, right? You sometimes yawn *after* a good night's sleep or when you're bored, anxious or hungry. Some chasmologists (yawn scientists) think yawning draws in colder air from outside to cool the brain, not by much but perhaps enough to improve brain performance. There are other theories, too . . .

Catching Yawns

Many people who see or hear a yawn suddenly find themselves yawning. Is this a leftover trait from our past before we could talk? Could it be a way of getting every prehistoric person in a group to go to bed at the same time? Or, if yawning really does clean away sleepy chemicals from the brain, is it to help make everyone more alert?

Wake Up!

The swift blast of air taken in by a yawn followed by slow breathing out may actually make you more alert. Atten-SHUN! The yawn might stimulate the special fluid your brain sits in, causing it to wash away chemicals that make you feel sleepy.

WHY ARE WE TICKLISH?

We're ticklish in two different ways – but we only understand one of them. When an object, such as a feather, is drawn lightly across your skin, light-touch sensors in the skin, called Meissner's corpuscles, react. You then feel an itchy-ticklish sensation as your brain is alerted that you're being touched.

Giggly Gargalesis

The second form of ticklishness is called *gargalesis* (try saying that with the giggles!). It causes uncontrollable, giggly laughter – whether you're enjoying being tickled or not. Could it have evolved as a survival instinct to protect vulnerable body parts, such as your stomach or neck? Perhaps it developed to encourage bonding between family groups. We just don't know.

DIY Tickling

One thing we *do* know is that you cannot truly tickle yourself – try it! A section of your brain called the *cerebellum* keeps track of all your body parts and tips off the rest of your brain, which then makes your own touch register as less tickly.

HANDY PUZZLERS

A few lucky people are ambidextrous – equally skilled at using both their left and right hands. Most of us, though, have one dominant hand – the one we're most comfortable writing and grasping with. But why do we have a dominant hand at all? And why are roughly only one in ten people left-handed?

Playing Favorites

Using just the one hand for a task might mean it frees up more of your brain to concentrate on other things. One-handedness could also be an advantage when rehearsing and practicing skills. You don't waste time teaching both hands to do something – you just focus on one hand getting it right.

Is Left-handedness Genetic?

Scientists think you may inherit left-handedness, but it's far from guaranteed. In fact, studies show there's only a 25 percent chance you'll be a lefty even if both your parents are. Is there a single gene responsible? It looks unlikely as scientists have already identified more than 30 which could play a part. Perhaps it's not genetic at all but caused by chemicals released during pregnancy.

Not Just Hands

You also have a dominant eye. Form a small triangle with your fingers and thumbs. Use it to frame an object in the distance, such as a clock. Close your left eye. If the object moves partly or completely out of the triangle, then your dominant eye is your left one. If it is still in the frame, then it's your right eye.

Outnumbered

Having a mix of righties and lefties may be a smart evolutionary move to ensure skills and abilities are shared, but why isn't the split even? Other species are also right- or left-handed, but the split is usually even, not 90–10 as it is with humans. Why are we the only species with such a strong right-hand bias?

Forced to Change

Society cruelly forced some people in the past to switch to using their right hand because lefties weren't trusted. Even the word left comes from the Anglo-Saxon or Germanic word "lyft," meaning "weak" or "broken." Despite geniuses such as Leonardo da Vinci and Marie Curie being lefties, some countries made left-handed writing a crime or banned writing this way in schools. But these laws and rules still don't explain the 90–10 split . . . and studies of prehistoric humans show there have always been far more righties than lefties.

THE STRANGEST SENSE

Smell is probably your least thought-about sense, the most underrated . . . and the most mysterious. We know that odor molecules, responsible for smells, interact with small patches inside the back of our nostrils, which contain odor receptor cells. But we've not been able to sniff out precisely how human brains identify so many different smells and why people's sense of smell vary.

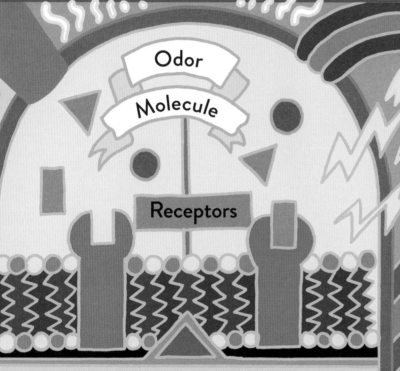

Odor Molecule

Receptors

Smell Shapes

Some scientists think that smell works because each odor molecule has a different shape that fits into a particular odor receptor cell in your nose. A good fit triggers the receptor to send signals to the brain. But other scientists think this theory stinks! They wonder how some molecules with almost identical shapes can have very different smells. For example, there's only the smallest difference between the odor molecule of freshly cut grass and the stink of rotten eggs.

Another problem not to be sniffed at is that our noses contain around 350–400 different odor receptors, far less than the number of smells we can detect. Perhaps the odor receptors work together in combination to identify a greater range of smells.

Why is Smell So Hard to Analyze?

Part of the problem is the sheer number and complexity of odor molecules. A strawberry is made up of 350 different substances and some coffees are formed from more than 800! We don't know how all these chemicals contribute to a smell or how your nose and brain identify them together as a single smell.

Smelling Colors

Some people have a condition called *synaesthesia* where they experience senses differently to most people. They might find they can smell colors or sounds. Scientists are unsure how this occurs and whether it's a genetic condition or something from early childhood. Is it due to a brain that has developed differently or down to some brain cells making too many (or not enough) connections?

How Many Smells Can We Detect?

The simple answer is we don't know . . . Figures vary from ten thousand to one trillion (1,000,000,000,000). If you wanted to smell a trillion smells, one each second, it would take you 31,709 years and nine months!

DOES THE APPENDIX DO ANYTHING?

The appendix is a small, tube-shaped pouch attached to your large intestine, like a short cul-de-sac branching off a big main road. For decades it was thought of as a vestigial organ. This is a body part humans have evolved to no longer use. We have others, such as the muscles that let you wiggle your ears!

The only time people tend to think about their appendix is if it has to be removed. When it's gone, nothing much seems to change, supporting the idea that it's pretty pointless. But scientists are now taking a serious second look at this humble organ.

Infection Instructor

Some think the appendix has something to do with a person's immune system. It may train white blood cells (which tackle infections) to recognize good and bad microbes when you are very young or even growing in the womb.

Microbe Motel

The appendix might store gut-friendly bacteria. When you have certain illnesses, such as a severe diarrhea, a lot of the friendly bacteria that help you digest food and avoid infections are flushed out of your intestines with poo. Yet, in most people, these friendly bacteria return. Bacteria tend to reproduce quickly, but could the appendix give your gut a helping hand by releasing its stash of human-friendly microbes?

WHY DO WE GET HICCUPS?

Everyone hiccups, from senior citizens to unborn babies. Poor Charles Osborne in the United States hiccupped continuously for 68 years (1922–1990)!

We know the mechanics of a hiccup. It's a spasm of your diaphragm – the sheet of stretchy muscle below your lungs. It suddenly tightens and moves downwards, drawing in air in between your breaths. As it does this, a little movable lid that can stop food and drink entering your windpipe snaps shut. This lid is called the epiglottis and its slamming shut produces that annoying "hic!" sound.

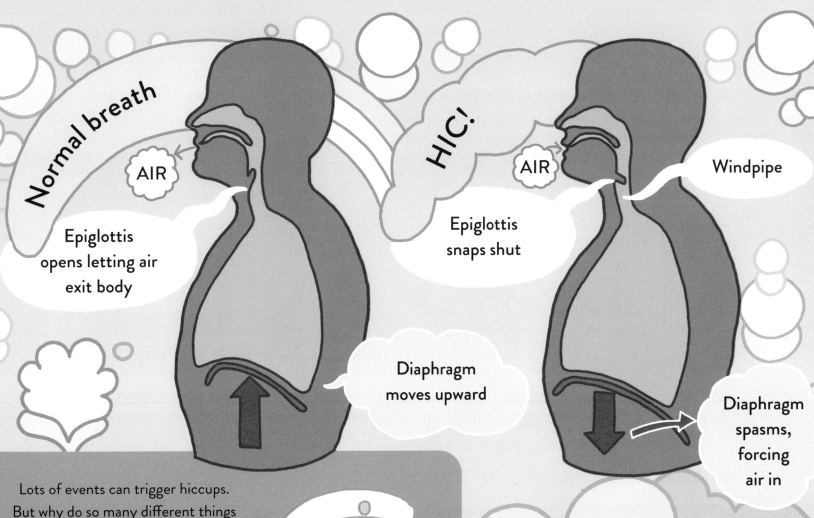

Normal breath

AIR

Epiglottis opens letting air exit body

Diaphragm moves upward

HIC!

AIR

Windpipe

Epiglottis snaps shut

Diaphragm spasms, forcing air in

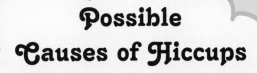

Lots of events can trigger hiccups. But why do so many different things end with the same response? We also don't know what causes the diaphragm to suddenly contract or why most hiccup attacks only last minutes, but some go on for days, weeks or, in the unlucky case of Charles Osborne's case, years.

Possible Causes of Hiccups

Stress	Meningitis
Excitement	Fizzy drinks
Diabetes	Stroke

MEMORIES ARE MADE OF THIS

From recalling names, dates and faces to repeating learned skills, you rely on your memory every day. Neuroscientists think that memories are stored not in one place like a giant disk drive, but throughout the brain, which contains 86 billion neurons (brain cells).

Who's in Charge?

Current thinking is that your memories are held in connections between neurons called synapses. Each neuron can make up to ten thousand connections, giving your brain serious storage capacity! But what's in charge of directing where each memory goes and how it's distributed among the connections? A small part of your brain called the *hippocampus* might be responsible, but it's such a big task for such a small thing.

Hippocampus

What Format?

How are memories held in those connections? Are they stored chemically, like hormones, or are they – like nerve signals – tiny spikes of electricity? If electric, how do tiny changes in electrical voltage describe complex memories, such as all the different feelings you've experienced with your sibling? And how do same-sized voltages in different parts of the brain conjure up completely different memories? It's enough to melt your brain!

Memory Mystery

Your brain holds information from your senses in its short-term memory for 30 seconds or so. Anything it pays more attention to, it sends to its long-term memory. We don't understand how our short-term memory – which can only hold four to seven different things at a time – is able to cope when you're bombarded with information. Are we missing a crucial part of the memory-making process?

Declutter and Overwrite

Your brain spring cleans itself and updates your memories. Sometimes, it cuts connections between neurons, called synaptic pruning, to remove clutter. Other times, it overwrites existing memories, adding data from the present into your past. That is why some people can recall a past event, such as their sixth birthday party, but can only remember the party guests as they look now, not as they did then.

Perfect Recall

Why do we recall so many things incorrectly? Was the memory filed away incorrectly in the first place? Or have the neurons that stored it in their connections been damaged? Is your brain's pruning vandalizing other memories or is it just overworked and imperfect but doing the best job it can?

So many questions, as yet, remain unanswered about your amazing brain!

WHAT IS DÉJÀ VU?

Ever felt like you've come across something before when you haven't? A person, place, situation or object may feel spookily familiar when it really shouldn't. This slightly unnerving feeling is called déjà vu – French for, "already seen." Research shows that 15–25 year olds experience more déjà vu moments than anyone else. Freaky!

Memory Error

It might be a filing error, caused by tiny, occasional glitches in your temporal lobes. These parts of the brain help make and store memories. A few brain cells might misfire and accidentally label something you're seeing as a long-term memory from the past. So your brain falsely thinks what you are currently experiencing is also an old memory, making it feel strangely familiar. Science cannot yet explain why such glitches might occur.

A Game of Two Halves

The left and right hemispheres (halves) of your brain share jobs. The two halves are connected by a thick band of nerve fibers called the *corpus callosum*. This is your own personal information superhighway. Some argue that a bit of a traffic jam or delay on this highway could mean that a single event is registered as happening twice, first in one hemisphere then a little later in the other. Could this lead to your brain telling you that you've experienced an event before?

WHAT IS THE PLACEBO EFFECT?

A placebo is a "fake" treatment or medicine, such as a pill made purely of sugar. It contains nothing to change a person in any way. Yet, for some people, if they don't know they're taking a placebo instead of actual medicine, their health improves. This baffling phenomenon is called the placebo effect.

For a long time, it was explained as being "all in the mind". Patients expected the placebo would make them better because they thought it was real medicine, so they felt more positive in general. They might then downplay their health problem or learn to cope with it and report that they were improving.

However, studies have shown real changes to the body's chemistry and functions can occur when some placebos are taken. For instance, certain patients who were given a placebo they thought was real heart medication found their heart rate and blood pressure improved. Those physical changes actually happened. Astonishing! How and why remain a mystery, but if science can find the answers it could be handy for health in the future.

When you lay your head down on your pillow and fall asleep, who knows where your brain will take you. Teens and adults have around four to six dreams a night, children under ten have even more. Dreams can be super silly or can feel startlingly real. Some are wonderful, others are nightmarish, but why do we dream at all?

Taking Stock

One theory is that sleep gives your brain and body a chance to refresh and take stock. Dreams may be a result of your brain processing information, moving experiences to memories or making connections between different thoughts and events.

Trash Night

Dreams might be your brain cleaning up the clutter and taking out the trash. As it sifts through the thoughts and experiences of the previous day, the brain chooses what memories to chuck and what to hold on to. Could dreams be little glimpses of what's being kept or what's being thrown away?

Disaster Ready

Some people believe unpleasant dreams, such as falling, fighting, being chased or hiding are your brain's way of training you. It may be prepping your responses to potential threats in the future – although a 65-foot-high pink monster chasing you is pretty unlikely!

On the Couch

Dreams are possibly the result of your brain acting as therapist, helping you cope with emotions and troubles in your waking life. Perhaps, when asleep, your brain is more able to deal with feelings, make connections and understand emotions better.

More Theories!

There are many other theories, too! Dreams may spur creativity and help us solve knotty problems in our sleep. The continual-activation theory suggests the dreams themselves mean very little, but we dream simply to keep our brains active for use the next day. The reverse-learning theory reckons we dream to forget! It argues that there's so much going on inside our heads that dreaming helps cut some connections between stored memories to tidy things up and make it easier for us to recall important memories in the future.

WHY DO WE JERK WHEN WE FALL ASLEEP?

Have you ever been in bed, almost asleep, only to feel as though you're falling and suddenly jolted your legs or jerked your upper body upright? These physical movements are caused by your muscles contracting (tightening up), but why these jerks occur is a puzzle.

As you fall asleep or enter a deeper sleep, your muscles and breathing relax. It may be that your brain mistakes this as a sign that you're falling and sends alarm signals around your body. Alternatively, it might be to do with the change in orientation from standing or sitting up to lying down. But this doesn't explain why some people jerk when sleeping upright!

WHY DO WE BLUSH?

Embarrassment? Nerves? Guilt? We're the only primate that blushes. Scientists know how blushing occurs. Your body produces a hormone called adrenaline. This causes a chemical messenger called *adenylyl cyclase* to send signals to blood vessels in your face to widen. More blood then flows through them, creating those telltale red cheeks.

But scientists remain red-faced as to why blushing evolved and how it helped early humans compete and survive, if at all. Is it just a way of communicating, like a smile or frown? Some think it might be a submissive display – a way of showing you don't want to fight or be in charge. Other creatures, such as wolves, do this by choosing to crouch low, show their tummy or flatten their ears. But we cannot control when we want to blush. So how could it be useful?

Wolves crouch really low and, in an ultimate sign of submission, roll over to present their most vulnerable part of their body to the dominant creature to state "I don't want to fight."

IT'S JUST AN ILLUSION

You see with your eyes AND your brain. It's your brain that makes sense of visual data sent to it by your eyes. Your brain can be tricked into getting things wrong, though, by optical illusions. Scientists understand why many illusions work, but some remain mystifying . . .

Hats Off

Is the top hat wider or taller? Nine out of ten people will answer taller, but use a ruler and you'll find they're the same length. This illusion has baffled people since its invention in the 1800s.

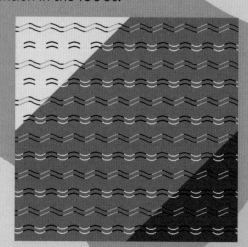

Curved or Jagged?

Look at the pairs of lines in the gray part of this image. Many appear to zigzag with sharp corners, but it's an illusion. All the lines are wavy lines with no corners. Somehow, this illusion by Japanese scientist Kohske Takahashi, tricks your brain's ability to spot corners as it seeks out the outline of objects.

These rows of tiles are slanting diagonally, aren't they? Grab a ruler and you'll find they're perfectly straight. Mind-bending, isn't it?

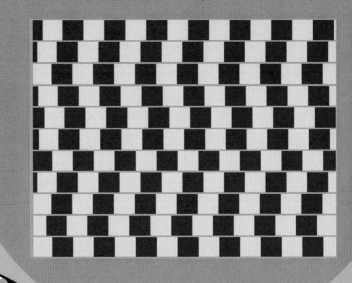

Moving Circles

Stare and you'll see some of the circles rotate even though they're part of a still image. One theory suggests that it's because your brain is processing the brighter parts of the image quicker than the darker parts. Another theory says it's because of the tiny movements your eyes make, called microsaccades, as they try to take in all of the image. Maybe it's a combination of reasons.

Not on Track

Which piece of toy track is largest? Looks obvious, doesn't it? Well, in fact, they're both identical with the exact same dimensions. Many explanations have been given – from our brain confusing 3D with 2D images to the top track's shorter curve tricking your brain into thinking the bottom track's outer curve is longer than it is. No explanation, though, has been accepted as the definitive answer.

EARTH ENIGMAS

SLIPPERY MYSTERY

Friction is the resistance one surface or object encounters when moving over another. Friction tends to heat objects up and slow movement down.

Science has long struggled to get a grip on ice, including how and why it's so slippery! One of the mysteries that people have pondered is why an ice skater can effortlessly glide across solid ice, even when it's bumpy, but not move as easily across other, smoother, materials. So what is oh-so-special about ice?

Under Pressure

The longest-held theory, popular for over a century, is that when an iceskate presses down on ice it causes the ice to melt due to pressure. This creates a layer of water on top of the ice, which acts as a lubricant and reduces friction, making the surface super slippery.

The pressure theory sounds good, but water doesn't normally reduce friction by much and you need a lot of pressure to melt ice. Scientific studies show that the pressure from the iceskate of a skater weighing 60 kilograms would only heat the ice up by 0.03°F. That's not enough to melt the ice and create a slippery layer . . .

Friction vs Friction

Could friction be cancelling itself out? Crazy, but (possibly) true, according to another theory. As the skater's blade moves it rubs against the ice and creates friction. This friction generates heat, which melts the ice and produces a layer of water. This theory might explain why ice is slippery when you move across it, but doesn't explain why ice still feels slippery when you stand still.

Ice, Ice, Baby

Another theory was stumbled upon by English scientist Michael Faraday over 170 years ago. Faraday discovered that if you take two ice cubes and place them on top of each other, they freeze together. Faraday supposed that ice's outermost layer was watery and didn't freeze unless it was pressed against another ice cube.

This idea was largely ignored until X-ray images revealed an incredibly thin layer of water molecules on the surface of ice. The layer is so thin that the water molecules act differently to usual. They move freely, rolling and tumbling over each other, creating a fluid, super-slippery surface.

At a close-up scale of 1 in. = 834 ft., Britain's coastline measures over 10,500 miles.

At 1 in. = 79 mi., the coastline's length decreases to around 2,100 miles.

At a scale of 1 in. = 158 mi., it appears shorter again at approximately 1,740 miles long.

COASTAL CHALLENGE

People are pretty good at measuring things. We know the precise distances between cities in a straight line, the exact height of mountains and even how far away the Moon is from Earth. One surprising set of measurements, though, escapes us – the length of a country's coastline. The puzzle with coastlines is the closer you look, the longer they get!

Coasts are endlessly jagged and wiggly. When a coastline is measured using a more zoomed-out map – for example, where 1 inch (in.) of map = 158 miles (mi.) of land – very little of the coast's jaggedness is shown. But a more zoomed-in map – for example, where 1 inch = 834 feet (ft.) of land – shows much more of a coastline's ins and outs.

And this continues as you get even closer. A 50-foot stretch of coastline may appear perfectly straight on a map, but if you stood on it, you'd see rocky parts jutting in and out. And a tape measure would reveal it is actually much longer than 50 feet. You would have to get down to a molecular level to get a truly accurate coastline measurement and that's not going to happen!

WHAT FORMS TORNADOES?

Tornadoes are violently spinning columns of air. Most only last five or ten minutes, but they appear with little notice. In that time they can be hugely destructive. In the United States, on average, there's just ten minutes' warning before a tornado strikes. This is nowhere near enough time to get everyone to safety.

We know tornadoes generally form inside a special type of thunderstorm called a supercell. Supercell storms contain a large, spinning mass of air, called a mesocyclone, which *sometimes* turns into a tornado but confusingly, not always. Many think something is going on inside the storm, perhaps at a microscopic level, which produces a tight, twisting column of air that extends from the clouds down to the earth as a tornado. But others think that tornadoes begin on the ground as small swirling winds, which are then boosted in size and speed massively by the supercell above them.

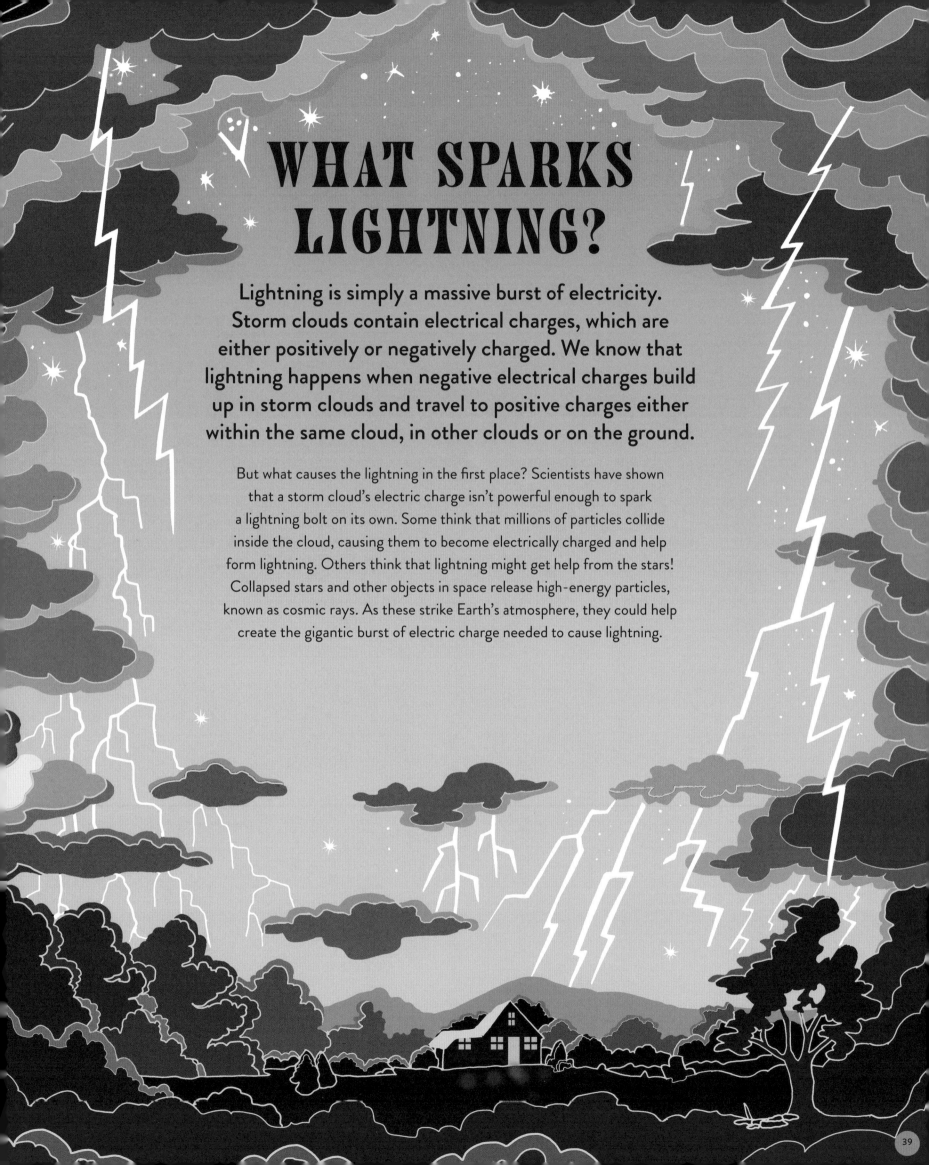

WHAT SPARKS LIGHTNING?

Lightning is simply a massive burst of electricity. Storm clouds contain electrical charges, which are either positively or negatively charged. We know that lightning happens when negative electrical charges build up in storm clouds and travel to positive charges either within the same cloud, in other clouds or on the ground.

But what causes the lightning in the first place? Scientists have shown that a storm cloud's electric charge isn't powerful enough to spark a lightning bolt on its own. Some think that millions of particles collide inside the cloud, causing them to become electrically charged and help form lightning. Others think that lightning might get help from the stars! Collapsed stars and other objects in space release high-energy particles, known as cosmic rays. As these strike Earth's atmosphere, they could help create the gigantic burst of electric charge needed to cause lightning.

QUAKE QUESTIONS

Earth's crust is split up into giant rocky slabs known as tectonic plates. These move half an inch each year but with massive force. As they rub and grind together or pull apart, energy builds up in the plates' rocks. An earthquake is the sudden release of some of this energy, which travels in waves through the ground. Earthquakes can cause mayhem, damage and destruction.

Ground shakes, cracks and damage all appear on Earth's surface.

The epicenter is the point on Earth's surface directly above the focus.

Earthquake energy travels as seismic waves.

The focus, or hypocenter, is where an earthquake begins underground.

How Do We Predict Earthquakes?

We don't! We know what causes earthquakes, but we don't know when the next one will strike. Scientists have tried to predict them by burying vibration sensors in the ground but without much success. Part of the problem is that many earthquakes start deep, deep underground (up to 435 miles down) – too far for us to examine easily.

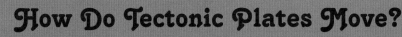

How Do Tectonic Plates Move?

No one is quite sure how these gigantic slabs of rock travel, but there's plenty of pushing and pulling over key theories. If we knew the answer, we might be able to predict earthquakes.

What Are Skyquakes?

These loud, distant booms in the sky aren't caused by earthquakes, but they do sometimes shake the ground. Explanations for skyquakes include sonic booms caused by aircraft flying faster than the speed of sound, distant storms or large explosions in quarries that sometimes travel through the air. But none of these seem quite right because these mystifying sounds have been heard where there were no storms or quarries and in the 19th century – long before supersonic aircraft were invented.

Convection Currents

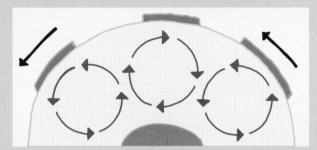

This theory focuses on the layer of Earth beneath its crust called the mantle. The mantle is warm because heat flows throughout it in currents. These currents might move and carry along the tectonic plates that sit on top of the mantle, like a gigantic conveyor belt.

Slab Pull

This theory suggests that where plates meet, one plate dives below another. Cooler than the mantle below it, the plate's front edge sinks, pulling the rest of the plate with it.

One tectonic plate grinds up alongside another plate.

Ridge Push

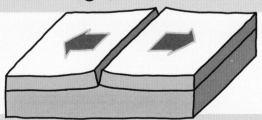

An alternative theory involves pushing not pulling. It imagines that as hot melted rock, called magma, rises up from Earth's mantle, it pushes the existing plates apart.

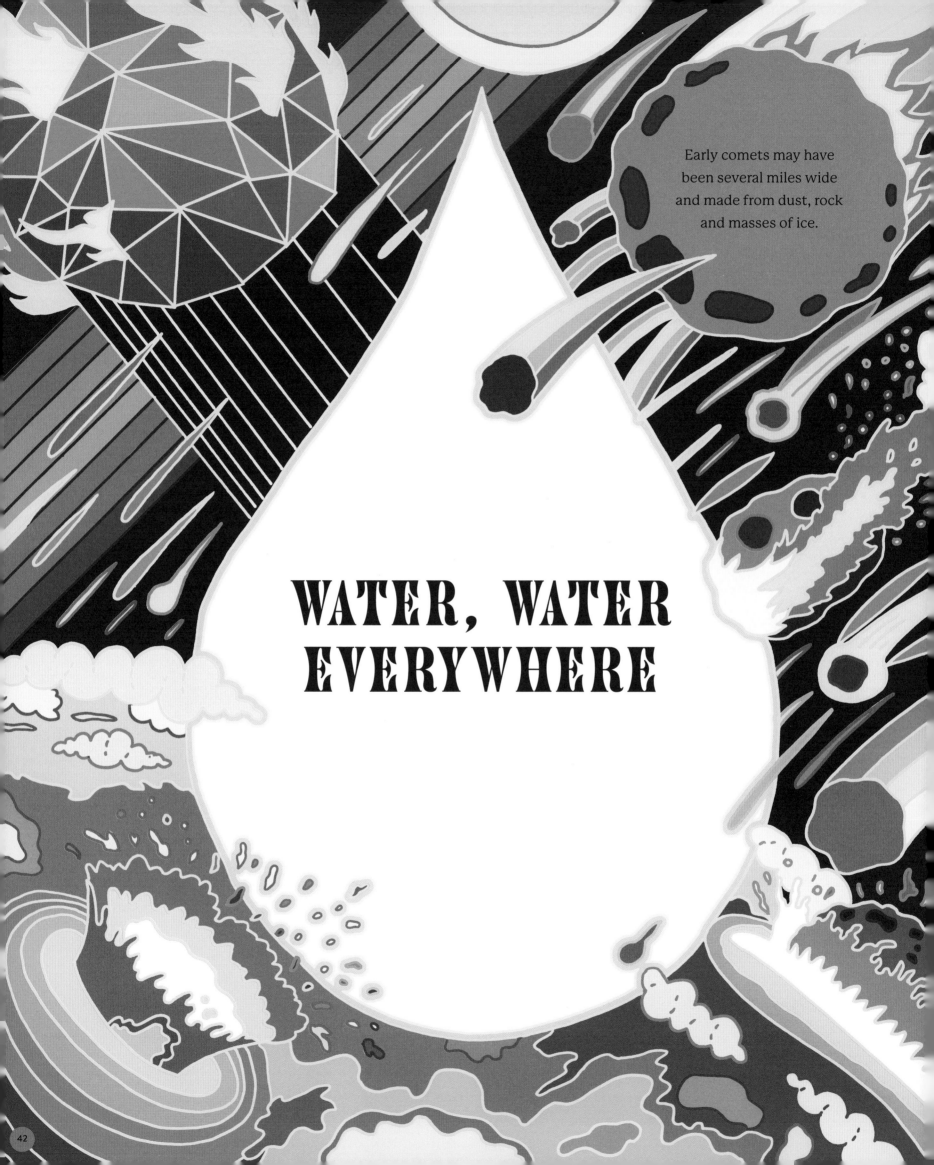

WATER, WATER EVERYWHERE

Early comets may have been several miles wide and made from dust, rock and masses of ice.

Water (H_2O) is absolutely essential for life. A total of 70 percent of Earth's surface is covered in it, with even more stored underground or frozen in ice sheets and glaciers. Astronomers are yet to find any other planet with as much of this precious liquid, but where did all our water come from?

Here All Along

Some believe there has always been water on Earth. Our planet was formed from parts of a dust and gas cloud called the solar nebula, which once surrounded the Sun. Maybe, the solar nebula also contained ice and some of the ice became part of Earth, which later developed into our rivers, lakes and oceans.

Mantle Moisture

Another theory also thinks the answer lies in the solar nebula. It wonders whether hydrogen was captured in the rocks that originally formed Earth. This hydrogen was then stored in the Earth's mantle (just below its crust) alongside oxygen-rich minerals. These may have later combined to form water.

Outside Help

Others feel that our young planet was too hot when it first formed to support water for hundreds of millions of years. So, it must have arrived later, probably carried by asteroids and meteorites from space. One type of these space rocks, called *carbonaceous chondrites*, can be as much as 20 percent water.

Dirty Snowballs

We think that Earth was bombarded with icy comets in the distant past, so it makes sense that these may have brought water to Earth. But some have doubts. Analysis of a few comets suggests that their ice is not quite the same, chemically speaking, as Earth's. But maybe ice on ancient comets had a different chemical makeup.

Hidden H_2O

Some scientists think that there's a reservoir of water deep within Earth's mantle held inside rock called ringwoodite. This pool may have formed when Earth gathered ice from the solar nebula or when water from asteroids impacted Earth and traveled into the mantle.

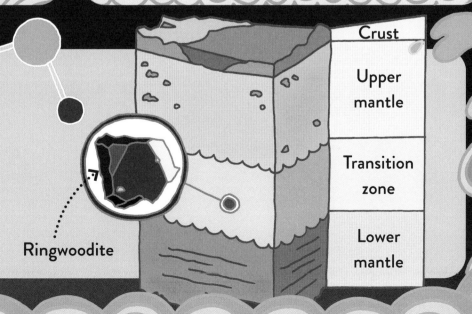

Ringwoodite

Crust

Upper mantle

Transition zone

Lower mantle

POLES APART

Did you know that 780 thousand years ago, Earth's magnetic North Pole was actually the South Pole? So, if you traveled back in time, your compass would point South not North! And it's happened hundreds of times before. This flipping of poles is called geomagnetic reversal. In the last 20 million years, the poles have switched on average once every 200,000–300,000 years. All this swapping has left scientists wondering, why do the poles switch places at all?

Earth's outer core is made of liquid iron and nickel. As it moves it creates our planet's magnetic field, which protects us from harmful radiation from space. The outer core moves because of a complex mixture of different forces. Some change or disturbance in these forces may cause the magnetic field to reverse and the poles to flip. But, because we cannot drill down more than 1,800 miles to reach the Earth's outer core (the deepest we've managed is 7.6 miles– just another 1,792 miles or so to go!), scientists don't know for certain if this is what's causing the poles to keep switching places.

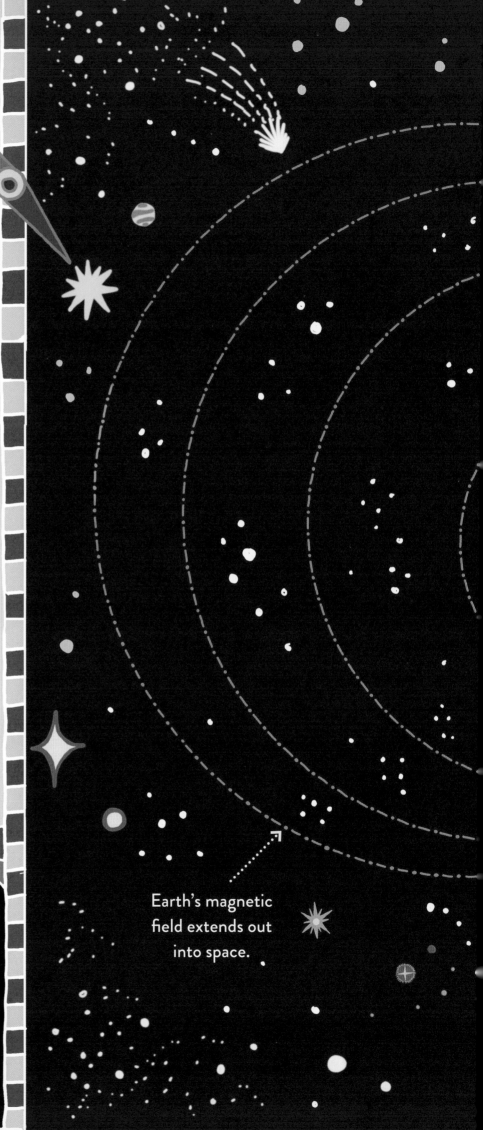

Earth's magnetic field extends out into space.

Magnetic North Pole

Geographic North Pole

Earth consists of four major layers — a thin rocky crust on the outside, a rocky mantle, a liquid outer core and a solid iron inner core right at the center.

Crust

Mantle

Outer core

Inner core

Geographic South Pole

Magnetic South Pole

WHAT CAUSED THE PATOMSKIY CRATER?

A strange crater, which looks like a giant eagle's nest with an egg in the middle, was discovered in a Siberian forest in 1949. It's more than 390 feet wide, 130 feet high and made of crushed chunks of limestone rock. Inside the crater lies an odd rounded mound, about 40 feet tall. Many explanations have been given for this eerie formation – from a secret nuclear weapons test site to a natural gas explosion.

Other theories include a volcanic eruption, but the crater lies in an area without any known volcanoes. Similarly, the theory that it's the result of a space meteorite impact is doubted because no meteorite fragments have been found nearby. Perhaps the answers lie beneath the crater, deep underground. No one is certain.

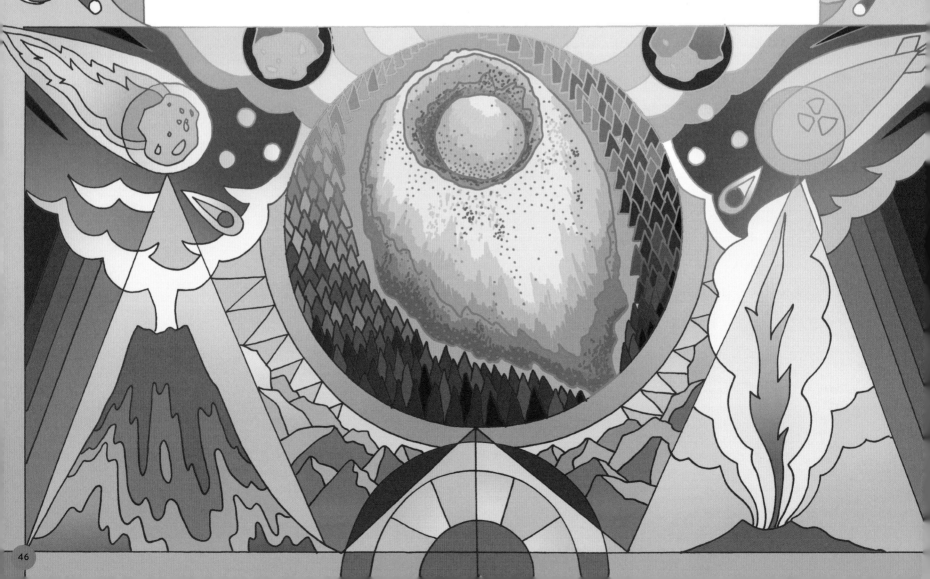

HOW WERE THE MIMA MOUNDS MADE?

Hundreds of gently rounded hills, most between 10 feet and 30 feet in diameter, are found grouped together in Washington State. Many explanations have been offered for this unusual landscape. Were they deposited by a large flood or shrinking glacier thousands of years ago? Or could winds have blown loose soil and grit together, a little like sand dunes, which clumped together around plants?

Another theory is that pocket gophers, which live in the region, made the mounds while digging their tunnels. But pocket gophers only live for three to four years and computer models show that each mound would take hundreds of years to evolve in this way. Could many generations of gophers have all worked on the same mound for centuries?

MIND THE GAP!

There's a great big gap in the Grand Canyon's rock record. Above it are 550-million-year-old sandstone layers and below it are ancient rocks billions of years old.

Throughout Earth's history, rocks formed different layers on top of each other, called strata. These have built up over time to create the landscape we see today. At exposed cliffs and canyons, the layers can be seen as bands of different colors and textures. Geologists study these to date rocks (younger rocks usually lie above older rocks) and learn how landscapes have changed over time. But puzzling gaps exist.

Missing Layers

This layered rock record is not perfect, though. Gaps, called "unconformities," exist, like missing pages of a book. A humongous 1.1-billion-year gap was spotted by explorer John Wesley Powell in 1869 when he was studying the cliffs of the Grand Canyon. Large missing layers of rock have also been found elsewhere. In all these places, rock layers between 550 and 3,000 million years old are missing. They're known as the Great Unconformity, and they're a big, rocky puzzle.

Snowball Earth

For many years, the most-accepted explanation could be found by looking at Earth 710–640 million years ago. This chilly period is nicknamed "Snowball Earth" because the planet was (almost) completely covered in ice. Maybe the enormous weight and movement of the ice eroded (wore away) many rock layers, removing them from the rock record.

Wind and Water

In 2021, geologists found that many layers of rock were completely eroded in Colorado, between 1,000 and 720 million years ago. That's before Earth became a snowball. This doesn't mean that the Snowball Earth theory didn't occur though, just that it may not have been the *only* cause of erosion. Perhaps giant slabs of land were pushed above ground during this time where they were more easily worn away by wind and water.

Mass Destruction

Around one billion years or so ago, a supercontinent formed, which was made up of much of Earth's land. Scientists call it Rodinia. Over the next 250–300 million years it split up into separate chunks. Some people think this break-up would have caused massive erosion and destruction of rock layers, which might explain the Great Unconformity.

The supercontinent, Rodinia.

WILD
WONDERINGS

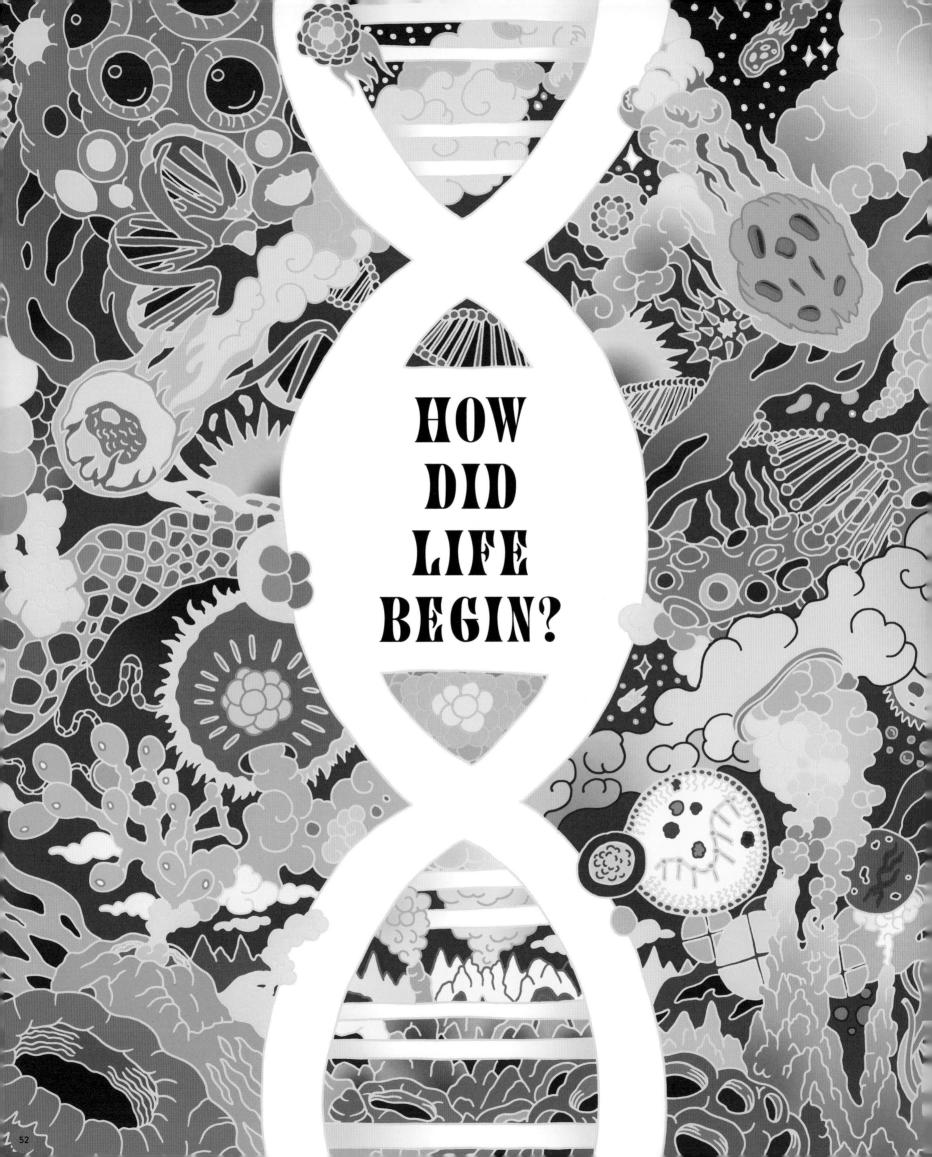

HOW
DID
LIFE
BEGIN?

Homo sapiens (that's you, me and all the other humans) first appeared around 300 thousand years ago. That makes us babies. The first life on Earth began more than 3.5 *billion* years ago. And all life is a mixture of complex chemicals, such as DNA, which help living things make copies of themselves. How these chemicals came about and how life first formed are amongst the biggest unsolved mysteries of all.

Primordial Soup Theory

Many think life began as the result of masses of chemical reactions. Elements such as carbon, oxygen and hydrogen somehow formed more complex chemicals such as sugars and acids. In this theory, these chemicals all existed together in water (making a primordial soup) and then somehow combined to form more and more complex substances, which eventually became the first basic living things.

Space Supply

Some ask whether there was enough time in Earth's early history (a few hundred million years) to create all the complex chemicals and processes found in life forms. They wonder if our planet had a little outside help with comets or asteroids bringing crucial chemicals from space to Earth. Perhaps this sped up the process and enabled life to form.

Alien Life

Others wonder if the first life on Earth actually arrived from space, carried on a meteorite or comet. This theory is called panspermia. Many think it's impossible, but a few think spore cells, which allow bacteria to reproduce, could have survived the long journeys and extreme conditions found in space, to reach Earth from elsewhere.

Where Did It All Start?

Where life first sprang up is also a mystery. The ocean is a popular choice because some scientists reckon the warm waters around cracks in the sea floor, called hydrothermal vents, provided the right conditions for early life. Others think it might have started deep under ice or on land in mineral-rich ponds warmed by hot rocks and volcanic activity close by.

AN EXPLOSIVE MYSTERY

For two billion years, life on Earth was pretty simple. So simple in fact it was mostly made up of tiny, single-celled organisms. But around 540 million years ago (mya), things suddenly got complicated. A great variety of complex and fully formed creatures, made up of thousands or millions of cells, started filling the seas, seemingly for the first time. They came in an amazing array of shapes and sizes and included the first-known shellfish, jellyfish and ancestors of insects and crabs. This extraordinary flowering of life is known as the Cambrian explosion. But what caused this massive leap forward in evolution?

A Warmer World

Some scientists think that life flourished because living conditions improved around the Cambrian period (541–485.4 mya). Before this, the planet was recovering from the Snowball Earth era (see page 49) when it had been covered in ice. Brrr! Perhaps the rising temperatures and sea levels or increases in food or oxygen levels in the ocean helped fuel this evolutionary burst.

All Change!

Did something change in these creatures' genes or surroundings to increase life? Maybe the arrival of the first complex creatures drastically altered what food was available and led to more competition for grub. Could this have spurred on life to evolve faster than usual as lots of new creatures developed in different ways to survive?

Soft Option

Scientists study and date fossils by looking at the rock layers they are found in. Creatures with hard body parts, such as shells and bones, form most of the fossils we find because soft body parts tend to dissolve. The Cambrian period was the first time lots of creatures with hard body parts existed. So, perhaps, lots of complex soft-bodied creatures lived before the Cambrian explosion, but we just haven't found their fossils in large numbers.

Wiped Out

Another theory is that the Cambrian explosion wasn't an explosion at all. It only looks like one because something happened which wiped away earlier fossils of complex creatures immediately before the Cambrian period. Could giant floods or glaciers have erased fossil evidence from 550–650 million years ago?

The largest predator in the Cambrian period was *Anomalocaris*, which was 15–24 incheslong, had large eyes and two claw-like limbs in front of its mouth.

HOW BIG?

From dinosaurs smaller than a chicken to ones longer than two buses, it might seem like we have all the answers about these prehistoric reptiles. But it turns out that a lot of what we think we know is based on guesswork. So, just how big (or small!) were dinosaurs, really?

Paleontologists (scientists who study prehistoric life) have to be great detectives. Using just tiny pieces of dinosaur bones, they must work out everything, from the size of the dinosaur to what it looked like. Occasionally, a complete skeleton is discovered, but more often, scientists are working with just a handful of bones. They use computer modeling and educated guesswork based on research and other skeletons to make decisions about their dino discoveries. But could their estimates be way off?

Many believe the current title-holder of "biggest dinosaur" is *Argentinosaurus*. They *think* it's more than 98 feet long. But they've only discovered a few vertebrae (spine bones), a thigh and some ribs. What if its complete, real-life skeleton was completely different from the scientists' estimates? Maybe it's much shorter than they think. Or perhaps it's bigger, heavier and even longer! And what about other contenders for the crown, such as *Supersaurus* or *Patagotitan*? The answers are hopefully buried below ground in the form of more complete fossilised skeletons, so let's keep digging . . .

Argentinosaurus has been estimated at 98–121 feet long and 66–110 tons (10–16 African elephants) in weight.

In 2017, a dinosaur footprint was found in Western Australia that was 5.5 feet long. The creature who made it may have been one of the biggest dinosaurs of all but no fossilized bones have yet been found.

DINO DOUBTS

Dinosaurs have fascinated people ever since people started digging their bones up many centuries ago. Despite a lot of bones and even more digging, there's an awful lot we still don't know about these magnificent and, sometimes scary, creatures.

What Color Were They?

What color do you think the *Velociraptor* was? Drab green? Brown? Purple and black stripes? Pink with feathers? The truth is, we don't know! Dinosaur experts are mostly in the dark because color pigments and skin rarely survive in fossils. In 2010, scientists did discover the remains of *Anchiornis* with bright red feathers and a *Sinosauropteryx* dinosaur's orange feathers. These hint at some dinosaurs being very colorful creatures indeed.

Bony Body Parts

Some dinosaurs, like the *Stegosaurus*, grew large bony plates along their back. Others, such as *Triceratops*, had huge bony frills surrounding their head. Why? Maybe they made the creature look bigger and more impressive to attract a mate or scare off predators. Or perhaps they offered some protection in fights. These body parts might have even controlled their body temperature by releasing heat.

Tyrannosaurus Who?

Mysteries surround the most famous dinosaur of all, the *Tyrannosaurus rex*. Were they covered in scales, furry fuzz or fabulous feathers? And what size were newborn T-rex babies? Let's not forget those tiny arms that couldn't even reach their mouths – what were they used for? And did these fearsome 30-foot-long beasts hunt live prey or were they scavengers who feasted on already-dead animals? There's so much more to learn before we could pass a complete T-rex test.

Pack Hunters?

There's a big debate in the dinosaur world: were they clever enough to work together as pack hunters or did they hunt alone? Scientists have found footprints showing meat-eating dinosaurs walking together in groups, but these footprints don't prove that they worked together to bring down prey bigger than themselves. The hunt for answers continues . . .

What Noises Did Dinosaurs Make?

The earth-trembling roars that dinosaurs make in movies are – you guessed it – completely made up! Many dinosaur experts think that some species actually made clicks, yelps or even cooed and quacked! Many hadrosaurs had hollow bony crests on their heads, and some experts think they blew air through these to make loud, deep trumpeting sounds.

EXTREME SURVIVORS

From microscopic insects and 98-foot-long blue whales to animals who survive the searing desert heat and those living on the pitch-black ocean floor, life on Earth is incredibly diverse. Some creatures push the boundaries of what we think is possible in their quest for survival. As a result, these extreme living things have created real-life riddles that scientists struggle to explain.

Going Green

Six species of New Guinea skink lizards have green bones, green muscles and even bright lime-green blood! The vivid color is caused by a toxic substance called *biliverdin*. These lizards live quite happily with very high levels of *biliverdin* – 40 times more than needed to kill a human! But how do the lizards survive and what is the toxin's purpose? Does it protect them against disease, make them less tasty to predators or is there some other reason? No one knows.

Vine Time

The amazing *Boquila trifoliolata* climbing vine from South America can grow its leaves to look just like the leaves of many other plant and tree species. One vine can mimic three different leaf types at the same time. Why? Possibly to avoid being eaten by herbivores. But without a sense of vision, how does the vine know what shape, color and pattern to match? Does it sniff out chemicals given off by the plant it wants to mimic? Scientists are unsure.

Short of Breath

Scientists thought ALL multi-celled animals used oxygen to make a fuel called ATP (*adenosine triphosphate*), which powers cells. But in 2020, a parasite called *H. salminicola* was found to lack the parts to either breathe or use oxygen to make fuel. How it gets its energy baffles scientists.

Hardy Tardies

Tardigrades are the world's toughest creatures. These eight-legged, 0.04-inch-long minibeasts can survive temperatures from a scorching 302°F down to the coldest possible temperature, -459°F. They can also survive without food and drink for DECADES and withstand five hundred times the amount of radiation needed to kill a human! Tardigrades have been left completely exposed in space for ten days without air and they *still* survived!

But why have they evolved for such extreme conditions that they will never face on Earth? This mystery has scientists pondering whether such conditions were once found on Earth. Others are perplexed by why tardigrades are the only known creature, out of millions of species, able to survive the vacuum of space.

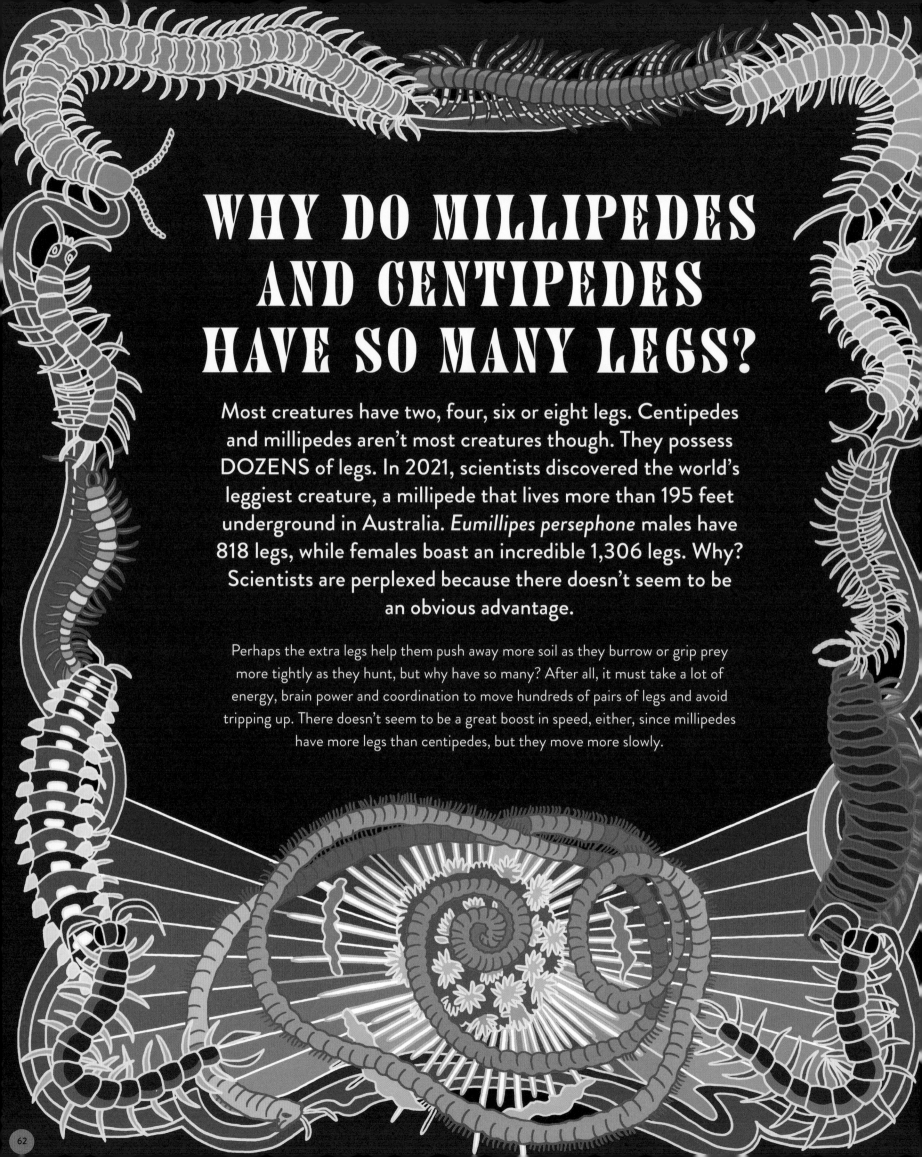

WHY DO MILLIPEDES AND CENTIPEDES HAVE SO MANY LEGS?

Most creatures have two, four, six or eight legs. Centipedes and millipedes aren't most creatures though. They possess DOZENS of legs. In 2021, scientists discovered the world's leggiest creature, a millipede that lives more than 195 feet underground in Australia. *Eumillipes persephone* males have 818 legs, while females boast an incredible 1,306 legs. Why? Scientists are perplexed because there doesn't seem to be an obvious advantage.

Perhaps the extra legs help them push away more soil as they burrow or grip prey more tightly as they hunt, but why have so many? After all, it must take a lot of energy, brain power and coordination to move hundreds of pairs of legs and avoid tripping up. There doesn't seem to be a great boost in speed, either, since millipedes have more legs than centipedes, but they move more slowly.

WHY ARE MOTHS ATTRACTED TO LIGHTS?

Switch on a garden light or flashlight outside on a summer's night and it isn't long before moths are flocking to and fluttering around it. Are they attracted to the light because it reminds them of other moths? Does the light muddle up their sense of direction or confuse how they navigate? We simply don't know.

Some reckon that artificial lighting confuses a moth, but electric lights are only 140 years old and moths have been behaving this way around natural flames and fires, as well as candles, for thousands of years. There are over 150 thousand species of moths, so maybe there's different reasons for different species. We do know, for example, that some moths don't like light at all and actually fly away from it, just to confuse things further!

MYSTERY MIGRATION

Life flutters by fast for butterflies. The longest survive for nine to twelve months but most experience far shorter lives. Some monarch butterflies live as little as two to six weeks. Others manage a few months. Yet, they go on incredible long-distance journeys through North and Central America, covering thousands of miles. It may take three generations of monarchs to complete the round trip with new butterflies born along the way. So how do they all know where to go?

Scientists have built computer models of how butterflies may find their way and *think* the monarchs use the angle of the Sun and a body clock built into their antennae to know how to head south. But monarchs can also navigate when it's overcast and the Sun cannot be seen. And you have to wonder how they keep track of distances covered, especially when they face challenges such as winds which blow these fragile insects off course. Equally mysterious is how does a brand-new butterfly, emerging from its chrysalis, know where on the route they are or when they've arrived at their final destination? Perhaps information about their route is passed down through their genes from generation to generation. It's a beautiful mystery known to millions of butterflies but none of us!

Some 100–200 million monarch butterflies migrate from Canada and the northern United States to central and southern Mexico for the winter, making the return journey each spring.

USA

Mexico

Clumps of monarchs rest on trees in a semi-dormant state during the winter to save energy. After all, they've had a long journey!

A monarch weighs less than a paperclip, yet they can fly 50 miles or more a day.

WHY DO WHALES BREACH?

Humpback whales are mysterious creatures. We don't know how long they live for or why they sing complex, 15-minute-long songs to each other. But one mystery is particularly baffling. They spend most of their time underwater, diving down to depths of 650 feet, but sometimes they rise, breach the ocean's surface and soar majestically into the air before crashing back into the water. Why?

Fish breach water to escape predators below, but an adult humpback whale is rarely hunted by other creatures. Barnacles, lice and other parasites, however, do attach themselves to the whale's skin. Some scientists believe that the friction and impact caused by breaching helps remove some of these pests.

Some think that the whales may breach to communicate. Their giant flops are loud but the noise doesn't travel far (unlike their songs, which can travel hundreds of miles underwater). So, breaching might be a way for whales to only communicate with their nearby group or pod. Others think that humpbacks breach to show-off to other whales or, maybe, it's just for fun!

WHY DO WHALES BEACH THEMSELVES?

A much less beautiful sight is when whales get stuck and become stranded on beaches, unable to get themselves back into the water. It can happen to lone whales or pods. In 2020, more than four hundred pilot whales all beached themselves in Tasmania, Australia. Some beached whales are rescued and survive but many sadly perish. There are lots theories about why this happens.

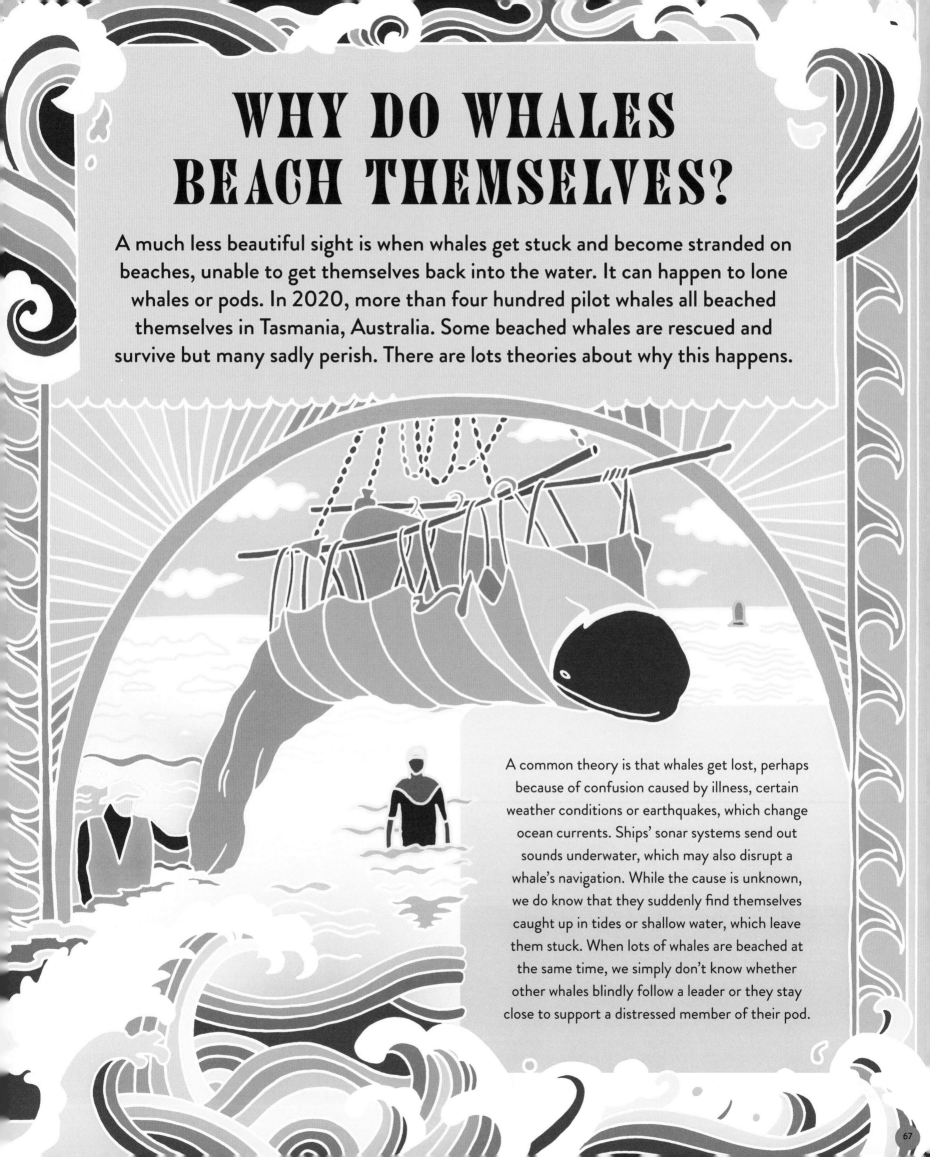

A common theory is that whales get lost, perhaps because of confusion caused by illness, certain weather conditions or earthquakes, which change ocean currents. Ships' sonar systems send out sounds underwater, which may also disrupt a whale's navigation. While the cause is unknown, we do know that they suddenly find themselves caught up in tides or shallow water, which leave them stuck. When lots of whales are beached at the same time, we simply don't know whether other whales blindly follow a leader or they stay close to support a distressed member of their pod.

WHY DO CATS PURR?

A cat's purr begins with signals sent from its brain to the muscles in its larynx (voice box). The muscles vibrate 20–150 times a second, and the purr is produced when air travels through the larynx as the cat breathes in and out. Kittens begin purring when they're just a few days old, before they can see or hear. Some think purring helps mothers know where all their kittens are during feeding time. But why adult cats purr is more of a mystery.

Most cats certainly purr when they're happy and content, after a good feed or when receiving a welcome stroke or tickle under the chin. But they also may purr when stressed, startled, injured or after a scary encounter with a dog. Some animal experts think that the vibrations generated by purring may have a calming or healing effect on our feline friends.

Found in the Amazon basin, the Caquetá titi is the only-known monkey whose babies purr, just like cats!

WHY DO CATS SIT IN CIRCLES?

Hundreds of social media posts and photos show the same thing: when an owner makes a circle on the floor out of a power cable, rope or masking tape, their cat seemingly can't help themselves and they go and sit inside the circle. It's fascinating behavior but an accurate explanation has yet to be found.

Perhaps it's just their in-built curiosity. Most cats know every square corner of their home environment and are simply fascinated by anything new in their surroundings. Others believe that it is to do with a sense of territory or security. Cats maybe feel that the circle's boundary somehow creates a safe space for them, much like how many cats love to curl up in a small box or round basket.

WHY DO ZEBRAS HAVE STRIPES?

Zebras and their striking stripes are a standout feature on the African plains. The stripes grow in their fur, which means if you shave a zebra, you would reveal their all-black skin underneath. But why do zebras grow these stripes and how come? After more than a century of experiments, research and arguments, scientists haven't found a clear explanation in black and white.

Some thought the stripes acted as camouflage, especially in wooded areas. But zebras spend most of their time on largely treeless plains. They rely on their powerful back legs to defend themselves or their incredible speed to escape, not camouflage.

Could each zebra's stripes help identify them to other members of their herd? Or do they act as an air conditioner? Scientists have found that on warm days the black stripes can be 27°F hotter than the white ones. This could create a swirling breeze along a zebra's body to cool it down.

The latest theory argues that they have evolved stripes to confuse horseflies and other insects, which bite zebras and give them diseases. Recent studies found that flies land less successfully on zebras and horses wearing zebra outfits (now, that is four-legged fancy dress!) than they do on regular horses. This suggests that the stripes dazzle or deter the flies in some way. Few natural world mysteries have stirred so much debate.

The largest creatures discovered in the past half century have all been found in the oceans, including the megamouth shark, 20-foot-long bigfin squid and 42-foot-long, 29-ton Rice's whale.

HIDE AND . . . BEAST!

Over the past few centuries, explorers and naturalists have roamed just about everywhere on Earth, searching for new life and seemingly leaving no stone unturned. Scientists in recent times have even used technology, such as space satellites, drones and GPS, to help them examine isolated mountain ranges and dense rainforests. There, they've discovered hundreds of new species, mostly insects and other small creatures. With the planet more photographed and mapped than ever before, surely every large creature alive has been found by now?

Well, some aren't certain the game is up just yet. They argue there are plenty of places to investigate further – from newly discovered cave systems to parts of the Amazon and Indonesian rainforests that have yet to be completely surveyed. In the past 20 years, new species of giant salamander, orangutans and whales – all pretty big animals – have been catalogued. And that's without considering the vast oceans that cover two-thirds of our planet. We've barely dived beneath the surface and almost everything below 650 feet has yet to be explored. Could unknown giant sea creatures be lurking in the ocean depths, awaiting discovery?

WHAT CAUSED THE BIGGEST EXTINCTION?

Around 252 million years ago, massive volcanic activity occurred in what is now Siberia, Russia. A huge series of eruptions may have tripled the amount of carbon dioxide in Earth's atmosphere.

The eruptions polluted Earth with harmful sulphur dioxide, which may have blocked out sunlight for long periods and triggered huge climate change.

At the end of the Permian period (252 million years ago), life on Earth nearly died out. A staggering 70 percent of all species on land disappeared, never to return. In the oceans it was even worse, with more than 90 percent of all creatures becoming extinct. Some think this "Great Dying" occurred "quickly" in just 30,000–200,000 years. Others estimate it took 10–20 million years. But what caused this mass extinction?

Carbon Culprit

A huge release of carbon dioxide (CO_2) from volcanic activity into the atmosphere may have caused severe climate change. Air and ocean temperatures possibly soared by as much as 18°F, proving deadly to most life. Some wonder if the extra CO_2 could have fallen as acid rain, killing plants and turning the oceans acidic, making them deadly for most marine life.

Gasping For Oxygen

Scientists estimate that at the start of the Permian period, Earth's atmosphere contained 30 percent oxygen (it has 21 percent today). Yet, a few million years after the Permian period ended, it was down to just 12 percent. Could this huge drop have killed off most creatures?

Great Impact

Could a comet, asteroid or large meteorite impact have caused the extinctions directly or by triggering lots of volcanic eruptions? While no evidence of a major 252-million-year-old impact has been found (yet), such events have occurred in Earth's history. An asteroid impact 66 million years ago, for example, wiped out all giant dinosaurs.

Methane Makers

A huge release of methane – a powerful greenhouse gas – may have caused the climate to spiral out of control. The gas could have been released when lots of ice melted or created by a boom in methane-producing bacteria.

Supercontinent

During the Permian period, all the land continents on Earth were combining to form a large supercontinent called Pangaea (this is *long* after the supercontinent Rodinia). As the land came together, it may have destroyed many shallow seas where much ocean life existed. It could have also changed ocean currents and climates. Critics, though, point out that it doesn't fully explain why so many land species died out as well.

COSMIC CONUNDRUMS

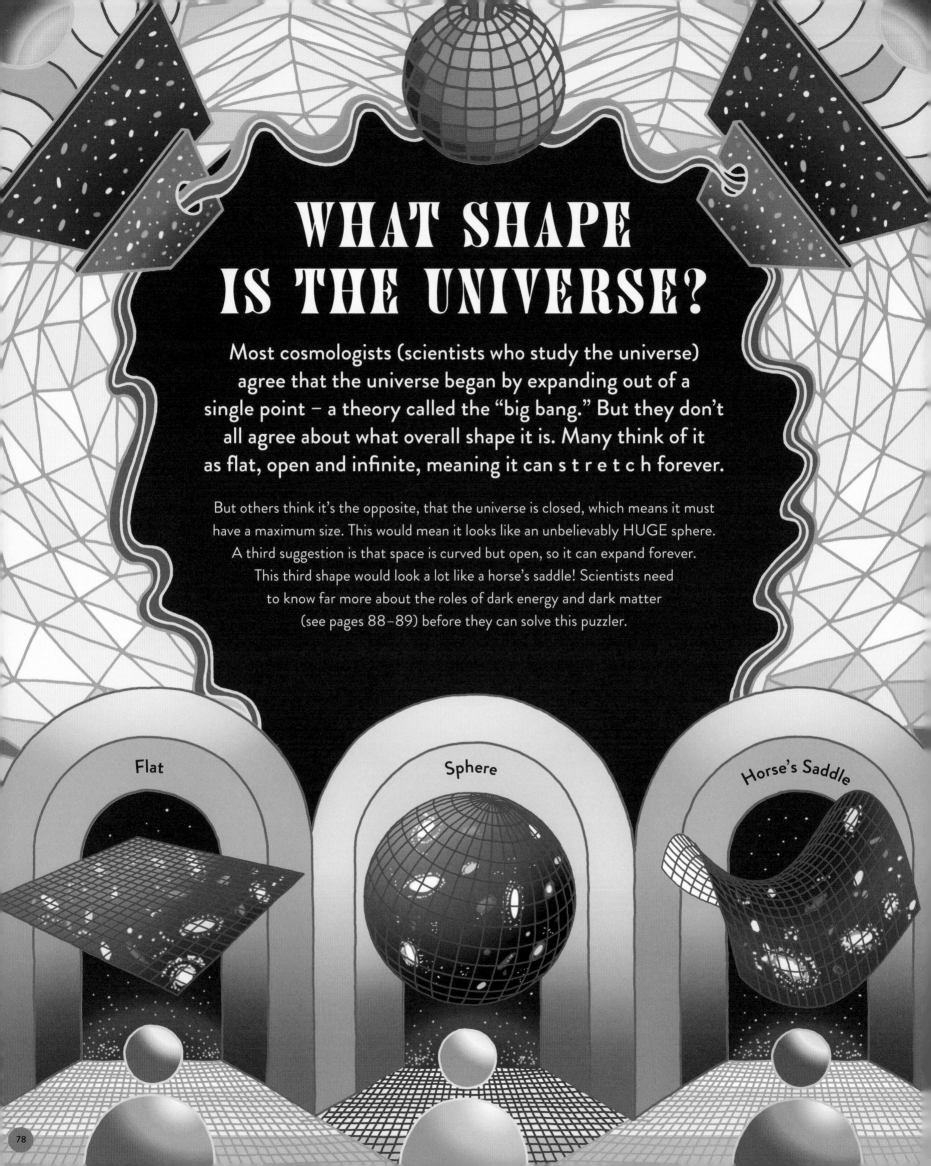

WHAT SHAPE IS THE UNIVERSE?

Most cosmologists (scientists who study the universe) agree that the universe began by expanding out of a single point – a theory called the "big bang." But they don't all agree about what overall shape it is. Many think of it as flat, open and infinite, meaning it can s t r e t c h forever.

But others think it's the opposite, that the universe is closed, which means it must have a maximum size. This would mean it looks like an unbelievably HUGE sphere. A third suggestion is that space is curved but open, so it can expand forever. This third shape would look a lot like a horse's saddle! Scientists need to know far more about the roles of dark energy and dark matter (see pages 88–89) before they can solve this puzzler.

Flat

Sphere

Horse's Saddle

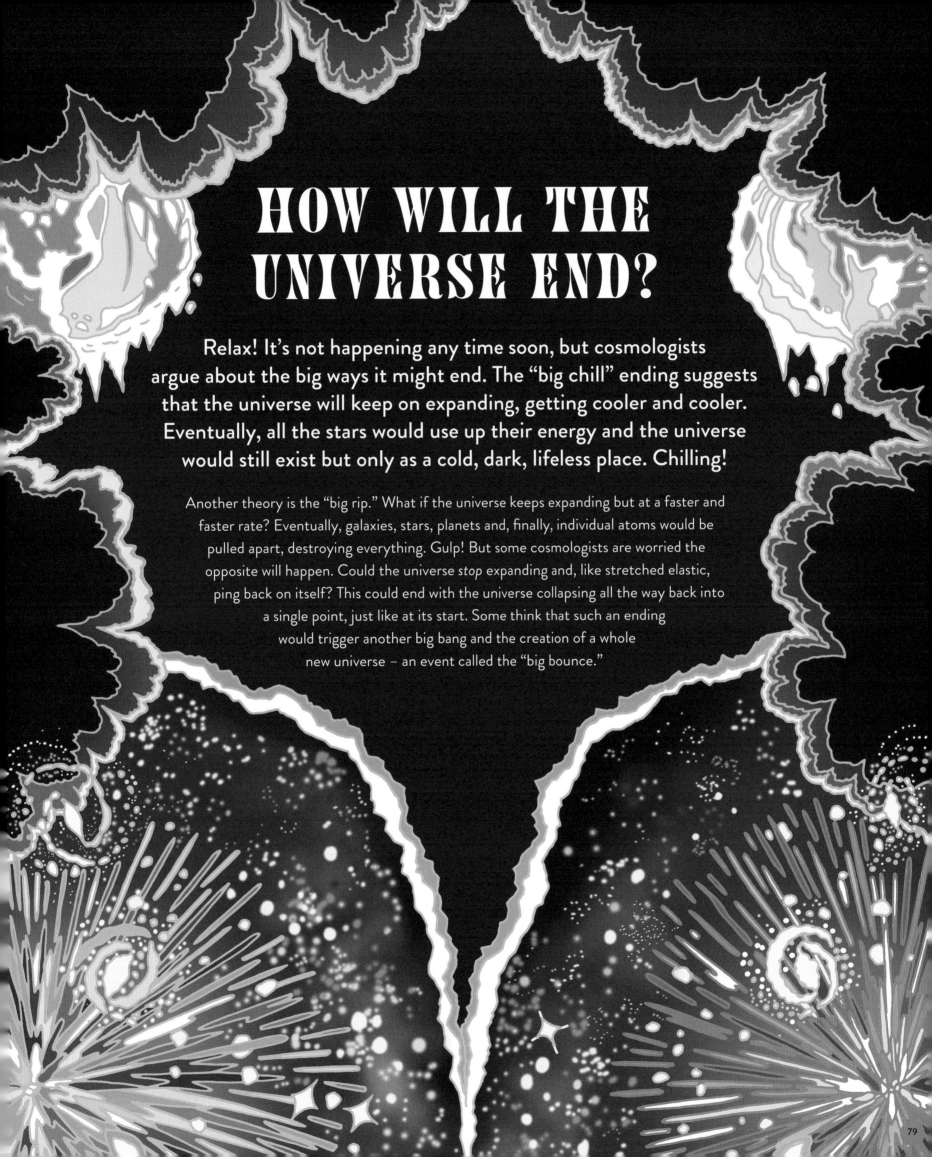

HOW WILL THE UNIVERSE END?

Relax! It's not happening any time soon, but cosmologists argue about the big ways it might end. The "big chill" ending suggests that the universe will keep on expanding, getting cooler and cooler. Eventually, all the stars would use up their energy and the universe would still exist but only as a cold, dark, lifeless place. Chilling!

Another theory is the "big rip." What if the universe keeps expanding but at a faster and faster rate? Eventually, galaxies, stars, planets and, finally, individual atoms would be pulled apart, destroying everything. Gulp! But some cosmologists are worried the opposite will happen. Could the universe *stop* expanding and, like stretched elastic, ping back on itself? This could end with the universe collapsing all the way back into a single point, just like at its start. Some think that such an ending would trigger another big bang and the creation of a whole new universe – an event called the "big bounce."

IS
THERE
ANYBODY
OUT THERE?

We know the universe is packed with trillions of stars. Our home galaxy – the Milky Way – contains 100–400 billion of them. Planets orbit around many of these stars, just like Earth orbits the Sun. So, if there are so many billions of planets, why haven't we been in contact with aliens from other worlds? Surely, we're not the only place in space that's home to intelligent life?

Rarer Than You Think

Maybe, planets like Earth are far rarer than we think. After all, conditions need to be just right. They need to be the perfect temperature, have liquid water, protection from space radiation, a breathable atmosphere and chemicals that act as building blocks for life. And then life has to evolve, which takes hundreds of millions of years. Some argue that the odds of all these things happening are incredibly small. But are they really one in a trillion?

You're Late!

The universe began 13.8 billion years ago and Earth formed 4.54 billion years ago, but *Homo sapiens* (us) are only 300 thousand years or so old. That leaves billions of years for intelligent life to have evolved, flourished and disappeared long before we turned up. Perhaps life has already existed and we just missed the party.

Far, Far Away

The universe is vast and we have only explored the teeniest tiniest part of it so far. Some scientists believe it is teeming with life right now, but it's all so far away that we simply haven't spotted each other yet. Hiya! After all, 40 years ago, no one on Earth had ever viewed a planet outside our solar system. Today, we know of more than five thousand of these exoplanets, meaning there's billions more still to find.

Not So Special

Far from being special, Earth and its inhabitants may be so primitive compared to other life that super-intelligent civilizations may have simply not bothered with us. Alternatively, they may have contacted us in the past but we lacked, and maybe still lack, the technology to receive and understand their messages.

People have sent gold records into space, containing maps and greetings in 55 languages, transmitted radio signals of our location and used giant radio dishes to gather signals from space. Is there anything else we can do?

PLANET PUZZLERS

The solar system may be our backyard in space, but there's still so much of it left to explore. There's hundreds of moons, thousands of asteroids and seven planets we call neighbors, all asking plenty of unanswered questions.

Why Is the Sun's Atmosphere Hotter Than Its Surface?

The surface of hot things is usually hotter than the space that surrounds them. With the Sun, though, it's confusingly the other way round. Its outer, visible surface is called the photosphere and is around 10,000°F. That's hot. But its outer atmosphere (the corona) is over 2,000,000°F (that's two million degrees Fahrenheit!), making it a truly scorching puzzle.

In a Spin

Venus spins on its axis in the opposite direction to all the other planets (well, except Uranus, which spins on its side!). It also spins *incredibly* slowly. One 360° rotation of Earth takes 23 hours, 56 minutes and four seconds, but Venus takes 243 Earth days to complete just one turn. A day on Venus is VERY long! Could Venus's thick, heavy atmosphere cause the planet to spin in reverse? Or, is it actually spinning the same way as Earth but for some reason it's upside down?

Is There a Ninth Planet?

Could a ninth planet, Planet X, be lurking at the edge of our solar system? This might explain why the orbits of some distant objects are unusual and bent out of shape. Computer models suggest that the gravity of a large planet about the size of Neptune might be responsible. Such a planet has yet to be spotted, and others wonder whether the gravity could be created by something else, such as a rogue object from outside the solar system.

NOT TO SCALE

Where's Oumuamua From?

In 2017, the first confirmed object from OUTSIDE our solar system arrived! Oumuamua is around one-quarter or a mile long, rocky and reddish. At one point it was racing along at 196,000 miles per hour – that's 11 times faster than the International Space Station. But where's it from? Astronomers plotted its path as coming from the direction of a star called Vega, but when it started its journey millions of years ago, the stars were in different places so its origins remain a mystery.

Oumuamua

STORMY THOUGHTS

There's a gigantic storm on the planet Jupiter that has been raging for longer than you, your parents or grandparents have been alive. The Great Red Spot may be 300–400 years old or older! It probably existed long before the invention of the powerful telescopes used to spot it, but for how long before remains a mystery.

But it's not just how old it is that has astronomers puzzled. The Great Red Spot is HUGE. At over 10,000 miles wide, it is 1.3 times wider than our entire planet. Yet, in the past, it was over 25,000 miles wide (three times Earth's size!). What is causing the storm to shrink so dramatically? Is it dying off? And what forces or phenomena can keep a storm going for centuries when most storms on Earth only last days or weeks at most?

A final mystery swirls around its wind speeds, which reach 400 miles per hour at the storm's edge – that's more than twice the top speed of a hurricane on Earth. These speeds are increasing by 1.6 miles per hour per year but no one knows why . . . yet.

The Great Red Spot is not always red. Sometimes, it's orange, rusty brown or salmon pink. Astronomers are confused by the changes in color and why is it red most of the time.

The Juno spacecraft solved one mystery about the Great Red Spot — how deep does it go? The NASA space probe measured its depth as about 200 miles.

HOW MANY BLACK HOLES ARE THERE?

A black hole is a point in space that's absolutely jam-packed with matter. Its gravity is so powerful that little can escape it, including light. This makes black holes *very* hard to spot. Instead, scientists find them by looking at how they influence nearby things, such as dust, gas and stars.

Stellar black holes form when a large star dies and its remains collapse in on itself. NASA estimates there's between 10 million and 1,000 million of these in the Milky Way alone. Counting all of those would be hard (and take a long time!) and our home galaxy is just one of many billions found in the universe.

Some scientists believe that micro black holes also exist. These may contain millions of tons of matter, yet be no bigger than an atom. If they exist, they would make counting all the universe's black holes close to impossible.

Black hole

Spinning disc of gas and dust

Matter is basically stuff — anything with a physical presence, from a single atom to a fridge, car, giant planet or star and everything in between.

HOW DO SUPERMASSIVE BLACK HOLES FORM?

Supermassive black holes (SBHs) are found at the center of galaxies. There's one in the middle of the Milky Way named Sagittarius A*. They're far bigger and packed with more matter than stellar black holes. Sagittarius A* is reckoned to contain as much matter as over four million suns. But how do these monsters form?

Too massive to be the remains of a single collapsed star, some think SBHs form when smaller black holes grow and merge together. Others think that they may be formed by a cluster of stars all collapsing at the same time or from dark matter (see pages 88–89), which could explain their huge mass. However they form, one thing is clear – SBHs are MASSIVE!

DARK MATTERS

Some astronomers are embarrassed. The reason? They're struggling to answer a simple-sounding question: what's the universe made of? The planets, stars and energy we can observe only make up a measly 5 percent of the universe. What forms the rest of it is unknown, and this is the BIGGEST mystery of all!

What Is Dark Matter?

We know what matter is. It makes up *everything* that takes up space (including you!), from the smallest atom to the biggest star. The more matter something has, the more gravity it has. Simple! The trouble is scientists believe there's far more gravity in the universe than there should be for the amount of matter they know about. So, where is the extra gravity coming from? The theory is . . . dark matter! This kind of matter doesn't give out light so we can't detect it, but scientists *think* it makes up a whopping 27 percent of the universe.

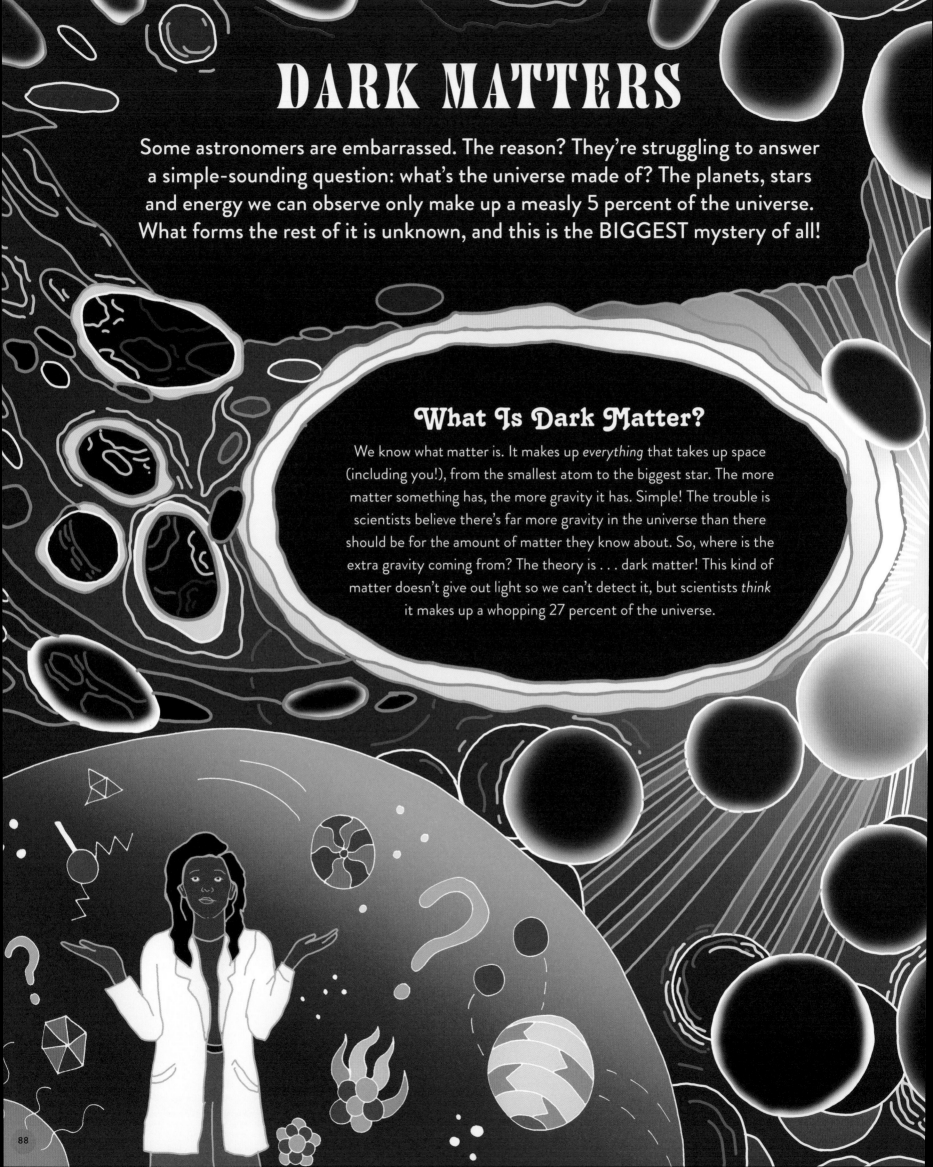

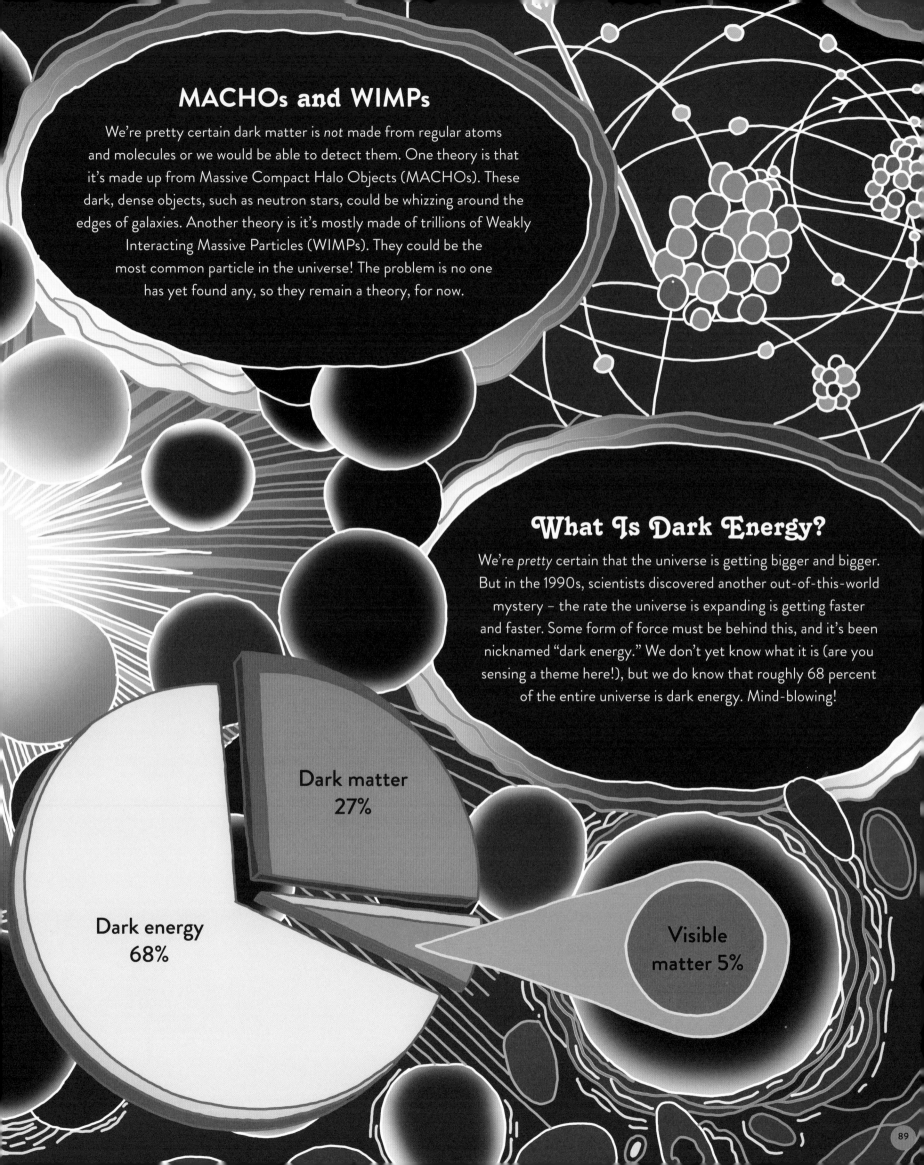

MACHOs and WIMPs

We're pretty certain dark matter is *not* made from regular atoms and molecules or we would be able to detect them. One theory is that it's made up from Massive Compact Halo Objects (MACHOs). These dark, dense objects, such as neutron stars, could be whizzing around the edges of galaxies. Another theory is it's mostly made of trillions of Weakly Interacting Massive Particles (WIMPs). They could be the most common particle in the universe! The problem is no one has yet found any, so they remain a theory, for now.

What Is Dark Energy?

We're *pretty* certain that the universe is getting bigger and bigger. But in the 1990s, scientists discovered another out-of-this-world mystery – the rate the universe is expanding is getting faster and faster. Some form of force must be behind this, and it's been nicknamed "dark energy." We don't yet know what it is (are you sensing a theme here!), but we do know that roughly 68 percent of the entire universe is dark energy. Mind-blowing!

Dark matter
27%

Dark energy
68%

Visible
matter 5%

TIME TRAVEL

Some ask, if traveling backwards into the past is possible, why haven't time travelers from the distant future come to visit us?

Do you dream of seeing living dinosaurs up close, visiting ancient Rome or checking out Earth in the future? Of course you do! Everyone's fascinated by time travel, but is it even possible?

Yes, in Theory . . .

In the 20th century, physicist Albert Einstein produced his mind-blowing theories about relativity. These state that time and space are linked and show how the faster something travels, the more time slows down for it. So, *in theory*, you could time travel forwards, sort of, by racing through space at (almost) the speed of light. This would cause time to pass more slowly for you. When you returned to Earth, you wouldn't have aged as much as your friends.

Too Slow

Many think practical time travel won't ever happen because our technology will never be advanced enough. To travel days, months or years into the future, you'd need to be moving really close to the speed of light, which is about 186,000 miles *per second*. So far, we've only managed to reach 119 miles per second, so we're an awfully long way off.

You Can't Go Back

Even if we could travel fast enough to go forward in time, many think traveling back in time is impossible because it would create unsolvable problems known as paradoxes. One example is, if you went back in time and stopped your parents from ever meeting each other, then you would not have been born. And if you were not born, how could you have traveled back in time? It's a total mind melter, isn't it?

Could There Be Other Ways To Time Travel?

Some space experts believe that there are shortcuts through space and time called wormholes. These might connect two really distant locations in space, allowing you to time travel by going through them. No wormholes have been found yet, so, like the possibility of human time travel, it remains just a theory.

Einstein's theory or relativity was proven by scientists who flew accurate clocks on fast aircraft around the world. The clocks showed time passing for them *slightly* more slowly — by less than a millionth of a second.

MISCELLANEOUS MYSTERIES

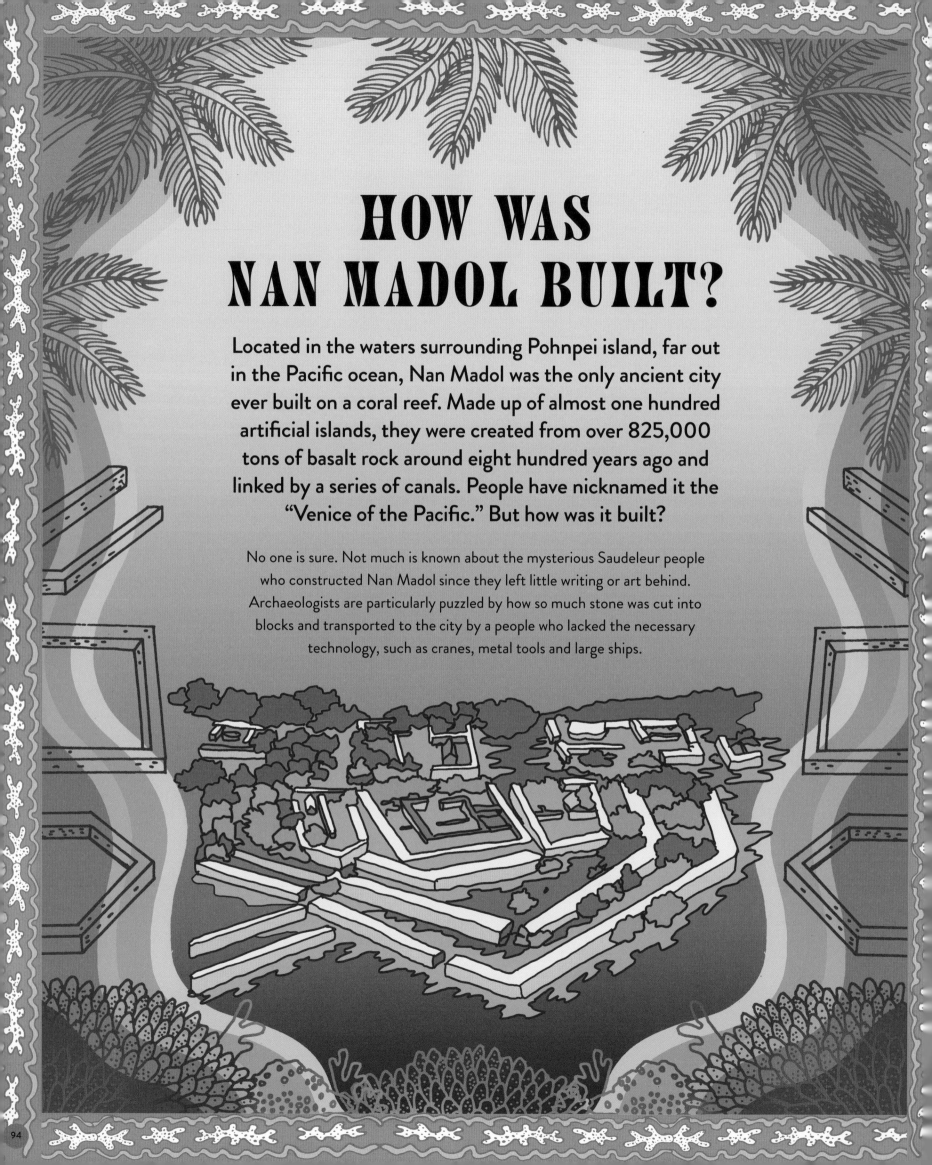

HOW WAS NAN MADOL BUILT?

Located in the waters surrounding Pohnpei island, far out in the Pacific ocean, Nan Madol was the only ancient city ever built on a coral reef. Made up of almost one hundred artificial islands, they were created from over 825,000 tons of basalt rock around eight hundred years ago and linked by a series of canals. People have nicknamed it the "Venice of the Pacific." But how was it built?

No one is sure. Not much is known about the mysterious Saudeleur people who constructed Nan Madol since they left little writing or art behind. Archaeologists are particularly puzzled by how so much stone was cut into blocks and transported to the city by a people who lacked the necessary technology, such as cranes, metal tools and large ships.

HOW WERE THE NAZCA LINES MADE?

In Peru, around two thousand years ago, shallow but very long trenches were dug to create lines in the desert's surface. Many of these lines were carefully constructed to form giant geometric artworks of plants and creatures, some larger than a soccer field. These images include spiders, monkeys, birds and a human with a large head like a helmet, who has been nicknamed "the astronaut."

Despite their giant size, the beauty of these images can only really be viewed from high in the sky. In fact, they weren't rediscovered until the 1920s when aircraft flew over them. So, how and why did the Nazca fashion these amazing artworks when they couldn't properly view them from the ground?

In the past ten years, dozens of new Nazca lines, figures and patterns have been discovered. Why were so many created?

UNCRACKED CODES

Experts have become pretty skilled at deciphering coded messages and lost languages. Some reveal fascinating secrets and knowledge that have remained unread for years. But not all codes crack easily. Is it because there isn't enough of the original language remaining or is the text just a hoax, filled with nonsense?

What Is the Voynich Manuscript All About?

In 1912, a book dealer called Wilfrid Voynich got his hands on a mysterious manuscript. It featured 240 pages of strange illustrations of plants, nymphs and text in an unknown alphabet written on very old calfskin. Dozens of specialists have tried to decipher it, often using code-cracking computer programs, but to no avail. Not a single sentence has been understood. Some think it might be a book about natural medicines, others think it was the work of Leonardo da Vinci and then there's the question of whether it is an elaborate hoax created by Voynich himself? No one knows!

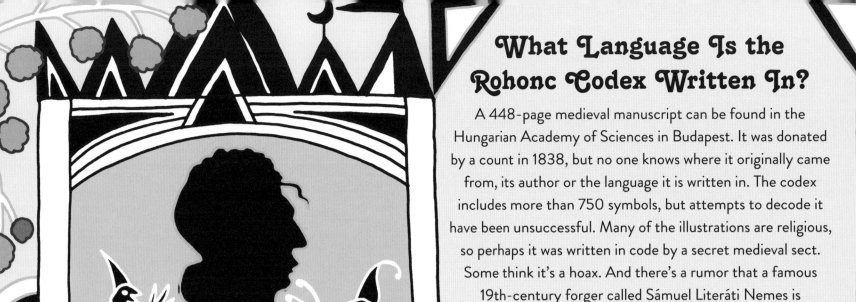

What Language Is the Rohonc Codex Written In?

A 448-page medieval manuscript can be found in the Hungarian Academy of Sciences in Budapest. It was donated by a count in 1838, but no one knows where it originally came from, its author or the language it is written in. The codex includes more than 750 symbols, but attempts to decode it have been unsuccessful. Many of the illustrations are religious, so perhaps it was written in code by a secret medieval sect. Some think it's a hoax. And there's a rumor that a famous 19th-century forger called Sámuel Literáti Nemes is responsible, but there's no direct evidence linking him to it.

What Is Written In Rongorongo?

Alone in the Pacific Ocean, surrounded by thousands of miles of open water, lies Rapa Nui (Easter Island). This tiny piece of land is home to more than nine hundred imposing stone figures called moai and a unique written language called Rongorongo, made up of little picture symbols known as glyphs. They are carved on to wooden tablets in careful rows. Less than 30 remain, but their meaning is lost. Could the tablets contain prayers, lists of families or do they form a history of the island? If ever decoded, could they shed light on the mystery of why the islanders built so many giant statues? For now – like the brooding moai statues – the mystery remains unanswered.

ARTIFACT ANOMALIES

Unearthed historical discoveries can be an exciting window into the past, revealing information about long-forgotten events, peoples and their culture. They can even change our view of history altogether. But some ancient artifacts have thrown up more questions than answers . . .

The Mystery Map

Part of a gazelle-skin map, drawn in 1513 and signed by Turkish admiral Piri Reis, was rediscovered in 1929. The map shows parts of North and South America and the Caribbean in surprising detail. Some believe the map's bottom part depicts Antarctica, a continent not "discovered" for another three hundred years. Was it lucky guesswork or had someone sailed that far south? And what wonders might the lost parts of the map portray?

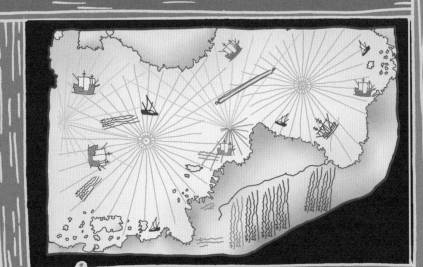

Antikythera mechanism replica

Antikythera mechanism

Admiral Piri Reis

Why Is the Antikythera Mechanism Unique?

Recovered from a shipwreck in 1901, this complex ancient Greek machine is the world's first-known mechanical computer. The 2,200-year-old device predicted the movements of the Sun, Moon and planets. Incredibly, it's one of a kind. No similar machines from that era have been found, and it took at least 1,000 years for anything like it to be built! But why? How was it made? And how was ancient Greek engineering so advanced, then seemingly forgotten?

Strange Stone Spheres

Hidden deep in the Costa Rican jungle lay more than three hundred perfectly round ancient stone balls. Ranging from small to very large, it would have taken months to shape the tough rock without metal tools. But what were they for? Did they mark indigenous peoples' borders, act as signs of wealth or represent the stars and planets? Or maybe they were used in ceremonies. No one knows.

Costa Rican stone spheres

Costa Rica

Roman dodecahedron

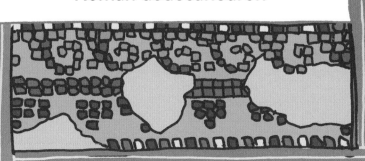

Twelve Sides of Confusion

More than one hundred bronze or copper alloy dodecahedrons (12-sided objects) have been unearthed in England and mainland Europe. They date back 1,600–1,800 years to the Roman Empire. Historians think they must have been highly valued, but as what? There's no written information about them. Guesses include: a child's toy, a good-luck charm, a candle holder, a weapon or a distance-measuring tool.

Roman Empire

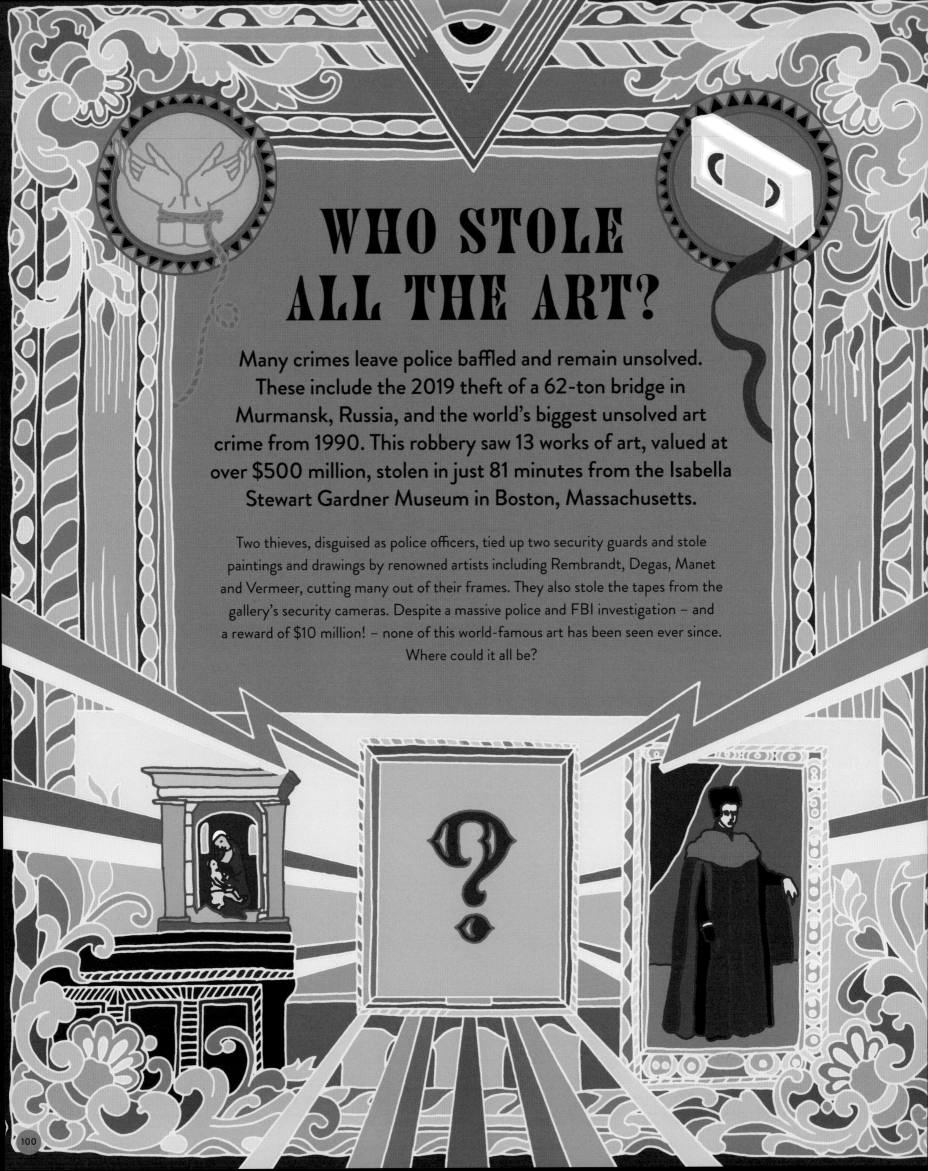

WHO STOLE ALL THE ART?

Many crimes leave police baffled and remain unsolved. These include the 2019 theft of a 62-ton bridge in Murmansk, Russia, and the world's biggest unsolved art crime from 1990. This robbery saw 13 works of art, valued at over $500 million, stolen in just 81 minutes from the Isabella Stewart Gardner Museum in Boston, Massachusetts.

Two thieves, disguised as police officers, tied up two security guards and stole paintings and drawings by renowned artists including Rembrandt, Degas, Manet and Vermeer, cutting many out of their frames. They also stole the tapes from the gallery's security cameras. Despite a massive police and FBI investigation – and a reward of $10 million! – none of this world-famous art has been seen ever since. Where could it all be?

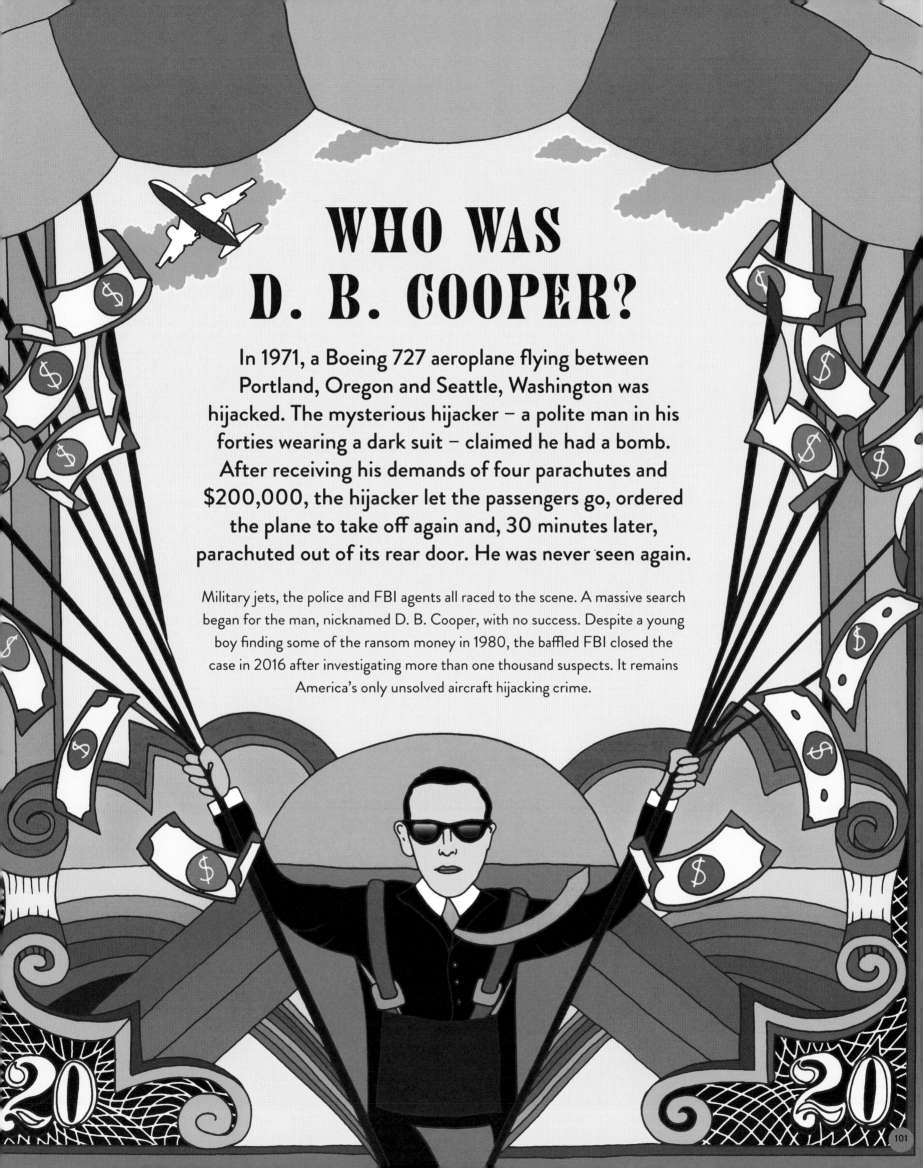

WHO WAS D. B. COOPER?

In 1971, a Boeing 727 aeroplane flying between Portland, Oregon and Seattle, Washington was hijacked. The mysterious hijacker – a polite man in his forties wearing a dark suit – claimed he had a bomb. After receiving his demands of four parachutes and $200,000, the hijacker let the passengers go, ordered the plane to take off again and, 30 minutes later, parachuted out of its rear door. He was never seen again.

Military jets, the police and FBI agents all raced to the scene. A massive search began for the man, nicknamed D. B. Cooper, with no success. Despite a young boy finding some of the ransom money in 1980, the baffled FBI closed the case in 2016 after investigating more than one thousand suspects. It remains America's only unsolved aircraft hijacking crime.

WILL AI TAKE OVER?

Robots marching down the streets and computers controlling your every move – the machines are in charge. Arrrgghhh! You've seen this sort of thing in sci-fi books, films and comics, but could it ever *actually* happen? Will machines ever be truly artificially intelligent and able to think for themselves?

Many machines have *some* artificial intelligence (AI). They can learn from and find patterns in information really fast and adjust their decisions and actions without human help. This makes them incredibly useful. Some can perform extraordinary tasks, from defeating human chess champions and detecting diseases to learning how to write poems and paint art.

Some argue that what current machines are doing, while impressive, isn't *truly* thinking. They are working within the limits of their computer program, written by human coders, so they cannot "think" for themselves, rise up and take over. Another problem is that we still don't fully understand how human thinking works, so how can we create machines that think like us if we don't understand how we think in the first place?

No machine can yet compete for all-around smartness with that cauliflower-sized lump found between your ears. Human brains have taken millions of years to evolve; modern AI has only been going since the 1940s. Given the amazing rate of progress so far, could breakthroughs in machine learning and increased understanding of how humans think lead to machines being able to properly think for themselves? For the moment neither artificial nor human intelligence knows!

Robots take in information about themselves and their surroundings using sensors. This is analyzed by the robot's controller, which makes decisions and instructs all the robot's parts.

WILL WE EVER MASTER NUCLEAR FUSION?

It's vital future fuels don't contribute to climate change. Will a suitable alternative be nuclear fusion? Many hope so. Nuclear power stations currently use nuclear *fission* to split the center of an atom to create energy. Nuclear *fusion* does the opposite; it *joins* the center of two or more atoms together. But no one's managed fusion on a big scale . . . yet.

Big Benefits

Nuclear fusion might fuse (join) the center of hydrogen atoms, such as tritium and deuterium because hydrogen is quite easy to get hold of. A big plus is nuclear fusion doesn't create harmful radioactive waste like current nuclear fission power stations. It also doesn't produce any gases that cause climate change. Best of all, for every ounce of fuel produced, fusion generates FOUR MILLION times more energy than burning the same amount of coal or oil.

NUCLEAR FUSION

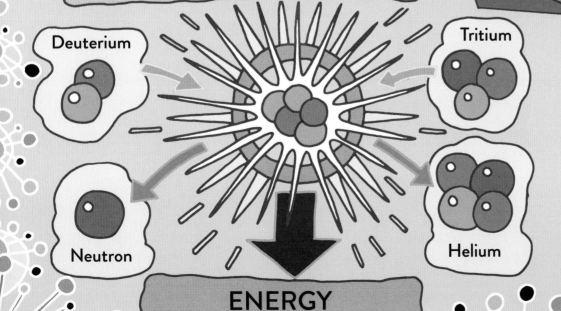

Deuterium

Tritium

Neutron

Helium

ENERGY

Huge Hurdles

The biggest problem with nuclear fusion is that it needs temperatures HOTTER than the Sun to work – more than 200 million °F. At the moment, fusion experiments are conducted in labs, but no one is certain whether we'll ever be able to build practical nuclear fusion power stations that can withstand the incredible temperatures needed.

WILL NANOMACHINES EVER DO VALUABLE WORK?

Nanotechnology is the science of building machines measured in nanometers. These are TINY measurements that are only billionths of a meter long. For example, it takes 80 thousand nanometers to span the width of just one human hair. Astonishingly, engineers have already built a handful of working machines at this mega-small scale, including pumps, engines and moving vehicles. Could we see millions of nanomachines performing vital repair work inside of machines or even the human body in the future?

Reality or Pipe Dream?

The problem is nanomachines have not yet left the labs. It is proving hard to manufacture them in large numbers or to get them to perform useful tasks. Some argue that they may never be practical to use. Others believe they might be common later in the 21st century as long as we can invent nanotechnology small enough to build the nanomachines! It's a big problem for such small things.

SOLVED!

Watch out: the Mysteryverse is constantly changing. Thanks to our expanding knowledge and improved technologies, new theories and discoveries are happening all the time. And these advances mean some big riddles and everyday quibbles get answered. Here are some mysteries than once baffled curious minds but have since been solved by science.

An Explosive Ending

In the icy Yamal region of Siberia, Russia, 17 mysterious, deep craters were found between 2013 and 2020. Some thought they might be from meteorite strikes, volcanic activity or sinkholes caused by collapsing rocks below. In 2021, Russian scientists found the answer (they think!). Large amounts of methane gas was being released by melting ice and frost deep underground. When the pressure of the gas built up, it caused explosions, which blew away the land, forming the deep craters.

The Windsor Hum

A deep, continuous humming sound was first heard in 2011 by people living in the Canadian city of Windsor. But no one could explain where it was coming from. It was only in 2020, when the COVID-19 pandemic forced many factories to shut down, that the mystery was solved. A steel-making factory's furnaces were causing the metal foundations of the building to vibrate, creating the low-level noise. Hummmm.

The Sailing Stones

In California's Death Valley, a dried-up lakebed known as Racetrack Playa contains one of Earth's most celebrated solved mysteries. Rocks, some weighing hundreds of pounds, seem to mysteriously move all by themselves across the surface, leaving behind a trail. Some travel more than 650 feet throughout the winter, but the winds aren't strong enough to move them.

In 2014, after years of investigations, it was announced that a thin layer of ice forms during the winter nights beneath the rocks. On sunny days, the ice breaks up into floating panels that push against the rocks. This push makes the rocks slide and move across the ground, leaving behind a muddy trail, which later hardens.

Slow Probes

In the early 1980s, NASA scientists were puzzled by their Pioneer 10 and Pioneer 11 space probes slowing down unexpectedly as they voyaged through space. This unexplained change in speed continued for decades. Were the probes encountering space storms, extra gravity or some other phenomenon that no one had predicted? Decades later, tapes of data from the probes were found under a staircase and provided the answer. Heat leaving the probes' systems and engines was pulling the spacecraft backwards – a phenomenom called thermal recoil, causing them to slow.

Blood Falls

A gruesome-looking waterfall of rusty red water flows out of the Taylor glacier and into Antarctica's Lake Bonney. Scientists previously thought algae was to blame, but they recently discovered that the color comes from iron-rich waters of a previously unknown lake, buried 1,300 feet beneath the glacier. The underground lake has never seen sunlight and its waters are low in oxygen but high in salt and iron, which gives it its blood-red color.

Cubed Poos

Wombats are the only mammals known to make cube-shaped poos! They use them to mark their territory, confident they won't roll away. Scientists have puzzled over how the cubes are formed for some time, but in 2018 researchers discovered the answer after experimenting with long balloons. They found that a wombat's 20-foot-long intestines has both super-stretchy and stiff parts to them. The stiff parts, when squeezed by muscles, help shape the edges of the cubed poo. The intestines also extract most of the moisture from the poo, which means they keep their shape.

The Bloop

In 1997, scientists detected an incredibly loud, deep and unusual sound underwater, not far from Antarctica. The sound, nicknamed "the Bloop," was heard from distances of more than 3,000 miles away several times that year but not since. Was it a ship's engines, an unknown military weapon or a strange, undiscovered creature? The truth proved less mysterious. The sound was created by an icequake, caused by an iceberg cracking and breaking away from an Antarctic glacier.

India's Iron Pillar

It doesn't take long for raw iron to rust once it's in contact with air and water. So the fact that a 1,600-year-old iron pillar in Delhi, India, remains largely rust-free was regarded as a metallic mystery. Was it evidence of an unknown advanced civilizations or even alien technology? The truth, sadly, is less exciting. Scientists found the pillar contained a thin outer layer of chemical substances, which help stop the nearly seven-ton pillar from rusting.

Fairy Circles

Dotted across parts of the Namib desert in southern Africa are patterns of 10–16-foot-wide circles of bare ground among the grass and plants. People have been baffled by what caused them, blaming termites, fairies and dragons, until scientists from the University of Pretoria in South Africa figured out the likely answer in 2021. The *euphorbia* plant, also known as the milk bush, gives off a poisonous sap from its branches. When it dies, the plant's sap kills off other plants nearby and coats the surrounding soil, stopping new plants absorbing much-needed water. This stops plants surviving and left the ground bare for many years until the sap breaks down and other plants can grow again.

GLOSSARY

antennae
Long feelers used by many insects to detect heat, air movement, smell or something else about their surroundings.

artificial intelligence
The ability of a computer program or a machine, such as a robot, to "think" and learn.

asteroid
A rocky body, smaller than a planet, that orbits the Sun.

astronomer
A scientist who studies stars, planets and other natural objects in space.

atmosphere
The layers of gases which surround a planet or moon.

bacteria
Tiny single-celled life forms.

big bang
The theory of how the universe formed from a single point around 13.8 billion years ago.

Cambrian period
A period of Earth's history stretching from approximately 541 million to 485.4 million years ago.

chemical reaction
The rearranging of the bonds between atoms of two or more substances to form new substances.

climate
The general weather conditions of a region over a long period of time.

climate change
Long-term shifts in a region's average temperature and weather patterns.

comet
An object made of dust and ice that orbits the Sun and, when warmed, travels with a long tail visible across the night sky.

computer model
A computer program, or series of programs, which simulates a real-life situation, such as a planet's orbit or a storm forming.

crust
The hard, rocky outer shell of some planets, including Earth.

erosion
The wearing away, usually of rock, by natural forces, such as ice, wind or flowing water.

evolution
The long-term process of change in living things, which often takes place over millions of years.

exoplanet
A planet found outside of our solar system that orbits a star other than the Sun.

forger
A person who produces fake artworks, documents or other objects to deceive others.

fossil
The remains or impression of a prehistoric plant or animal preserved in rock.

galaxy
A system in space containing millions or billions of stars all bound together by the force of gravity.

gene
The part of a living cell that contains information passed on from parents to their children, such as eye color.

geographic pole
A single fixed point on a spinning body or planet. It is found at the axis around which a body or planet spins.

glacier
A large mass of ice created by compacted snow, which moves slowly over land.

GPS
A navigation system that uses a series of satellites to give an accurate location on Earth. It stands for Global Positioning System.

gravity
The pulling force that attracts one object to another and prevents things from floating off into space.

herbivore
An animal that feeds on plants.

ice sheet
A mass of ice that covers an area of 20,000 square miles or more.

infinite
Something that is endless and has no size limits.